The diplomatic dilemma of Western Sahara

DM Ole Kiminta

Published by KBros, 2025.

THE DIPLOMATIC DILEMMA OF WESTERN SAHARA

First edition. March 22, 2025.

Copyright © 2025 DM Ole Kiminta.

ISBN: 978-1069323149

Written by DM Ole Kiminta.

Also by DM Ole Kiminta

How the Western Democracies failed the world
Supporting Refugees in their Homelands
Dissuading Global War Mongers:
Dissuading war mongers
La Libération Monétaire en Afrique
Canada Post: Management failure to modernise mail systems
Canada Post management failure to modernise mail systems
Canada Post: Management failure to modernise mail systems
Live to be 200
Aim to live for 200
Aim to live to be 200
Western democracies failed the world economies
Wrong foot forward: US-Canada trade wars
Canada begs to differ: Never a 51st state of USA
Tethered to the Kitchen
Nous ne pouvons pas être le 51e État des États-Unis
Nous ne serons jamais le 51ème état des États-Unis.
The Nephilim and the erosion of moral boundaries
Every human is an advocate for World Peace
The diplomatic dilemma of Western Sahara
Every human: Advocate for World Peace

Table of Contents

In loving memory of:

B. Nasreddine

A generous humble religious guy with a witty and pragmatic character of un-ending fortitude

A note to the reader

I must admit that this work has been difficult in the sense that I cannot fully lean with any side of this story because I am writing from outside as a Canadian. It is therefore my wish that the reader understands my point of view as an observer rather than a participant. I have family members on both sides and hence, my personal views become inflexible to skew to any side.

The diplomatic dilemma of Western Sahara

Chapter 1: Introduction to Western Sahara

The history of Europeans dividing people and lands has had many grievances over the years after they vacated out or released the lands that they had colonised. On the African continent alone, just like the Europeans landed on North America and divided lands and people without caring a flake in hell about the natives, so is the African's fate.

There are those that had closely netted tribes that had common language, culture and family ties like Morocco and the region of Western Sahara which the colonial power had named "Spanish Sahara". Then there are those like in East Africa where there are more than 100 different tribes and different religions who were herded like cattle into regions and became collectively as one country. others like South Sudan separated recently and look how many wars they have had in just within a few years. There are many reasons why trying to separate into small pieces of land is unproductive in many ways. In our current times, we actually live in a global village where everything is almost one. there is a lot that I could say, but it is only fair for me to let other writers who are better than me address the issue. My humble opinion is that people have to look carefully at leaders who advocate to separate and form governments that may not result in helping the people. Today, you only have to look at countries that have had a part of their country separating. In the case of the Sahrawian people, in my opinion, there is nothing to lose by staying the status quo because you are free and have freedom of choice, just do not chose the wrong individuals who have their interest elsewhere because they follow what the outside political players ask of them. again, my opinion is probably not everybody else opinion, but at least, in that way, I see piece in the far distance.

The historical context of Western Sahara's integration with Morocco is deeply rooted in the complex colonial legacy of the region. Following the end of Spanish colonial rule in the 1970s, Western Sahara became a contested territory, leading to a protracted conflict between Morocco and the Polisario Front, which advocates for independence. Morocco claims historical rights over the territory, citing its historical administration and the Treaty of Fez in 1912, which established Morocco as a protectorate under Spanish and French influence. This claim is bolstered by references to ancient maps and records that depict Western Sahara as part of a greater Moroccan kingdom, emphasizing the long-standing ties that have existed between the regions.

The question of territorial integrity is central to the debate surrounding Western Sahara's status. For Morocco, the integration of Western Sahara is seen as essential for maintaining national unity and sovereignty. The territorial claims are underscored by a sense of historical legitimacy, as Moroccan leaders argue that the division of the territory undermines the country's integrity. This perspective resonates with many Moroccans who view Western Sahara as an integral part of their national identity. The historical narrative of unity, which includes shared royal lineage and family ties, reinforces the argument for integration as a means of restoring historical boundaries and governance.

Economically, the integration of Western Sahara with Morocco holds significant promise for both regions. Morocco has invested in various development projects in the territory, aiming to boost its economy and improve infrastructure. The establishment of economic zones and investment in natural resource management could lead to increased employment opportunities and improved living standards for Sahrawis. The access to Moroccan markets and the potential for tourism development also present economic benefits that would enhance the overall prosperity of the region. This economic rationale is often presented as a compelling argument for why integration should be favored over independence.

Cultural and linguistic ties between Sahrawis and Moroccans further strengthen the case for integration. Both groups share a rich history of intermingling traditions, languages, and social practices. Arabic and Berber languages dominate the cultural landscape, and many Sahrawis identify closely with Moroccan culture. This shared heritage fosters a sense of belonging and unity that transcends political boundaries. The preservation and promotion of cultural identity under Moroccan governance could lead to a more inclusive society where both Sahrawis and Moroccans celebrate their commonalities, strengthening the social fabric of the region.

Finally, the security and stability of the region are significant concerns that underscore the importance of Moroccan governance in Western Sahara. The ongoing conflict has led to instability, which can be detrimental to local populations. Moroccan administration has been associated with efforts to enhance security and promote development, reducing the risk of violence and fostering a more peaceful coexistence among different ethnic groups. Additionally, international diplomatic support for Morocco's sovereignty is critical, as many countries recognize the importance of stability in the region. The alignment of shared religious and social values, coupled with Morocco's commitment to improving human rights and local governance, further illustrates how integration could lead to a more prosperous and harmonious future for Western Sahara.

Overview of Current Situation

The current situation in Western Sahara is characterised by a complex interplay of historical, socio-political, and economic factors that shape the discourse on its future. The region, long embroiled in territorial disputes, has seen competing claims from both the Sahrawi Arab Democratic Republic (SADR) and Morocco. The status of Western Sahara remains unresolved since the end of Spanish colonial rule in 1975, leading to a protracted conflict that has not only impacted the lives of its inhabitants but also the broader dynamics of North African politics. Understanding the current landscape requires an examination of Morocco's historical claims and the significance of territorial integrity in this ongoing dispute.

Historically, Morocco has maintained that Western Sahara is an integral part of its territory, citing various historical documents and cultural connections that predate colonial rule. The Royal Moroccan narrative emphasizes the historical ties of the Sahrawi people to the Moroccan kingdom, underscoring a shared heritage that predates Spanish colonization. This perspective is critical in the debate over sovereignty, as it frames Morocco's claims in the context of national identity and territorial coherence, which many argue are essential for the stability and unity of the Moroccan state.

The economic benefits of integrating Western Sahara with Morocco are increasingly evident. The Moroccan government has invested significantly in infrastructure projects in the region, aiming to enhance connectivity and provide essential services to the local population. These investments have the potential to stimulate economic growth, create jobs, and improve the overall quality of life for Sahrawis. Additionally, the integration could facilitate better resource management, allowing for equitable distribution of natural resources that are abundant in the region, including fisheries and phosphates, which are vital for both local and national economies.

Cultural and linguistic ties further reinforce the argument for integration. The majority of Sahrawis share cultural practices, language, and social values with Moroccans, fostering a sense of unity that transcends political boundaries. This commonality not only enhances social cohesion but also strengthens the argument for a shared national identity. Moreover, the role of religious values in promoting solidarity among the populations cannot be overlooked, as Islam is a central element of life and governance in both Morocco and Western Sahara.

Finally, the implications of Moroccan governance for security and stability in the region are paramount. The presence of Moroccan authorities has been associated with efforts to maintain peace and security, which are crucial for both local residents and the broader North African region. Furthermore, international diplomatic support for Morocco's sovereignty over Western Sahara underscores a growing recognition of its governance as a stabilizing factor. This diplomatic backing, combined with the potential for enhanced human rights protections and local governance under Moroccan administration, paints a picture of a future where Western Sahara can thrive economically, culturally, and socially as a part of Morocco.

Chapter 2: Reasons for Western Sahara to Remain as Part of Morocco

The legal foundations of Moroccan sovereignty are deeply rooted in historical treaties, international law, and the principles of self-determination. Morocco's claim to Western Sahara is supported by a series of legal documents and declarations that affirm its territorial integrity. The historical ties between the Moroccan state and the Western Sahara region can be traced back to pre-colonial times when the area was part of the Moroccan kingdom. The 1975 Madrid Accords, which involved Spain's withdrawal from the territory, further legitimized Morocco's claims by establishing a framework for its administration and governance, while recognizing the interests of Morocco, Mauritania, and the Sahrawi people.

International law also plays a significant role in the discourse surrounding Moroccan sovereignty over Western Sahara. The United Nations has recognized the need for a resolution to the conflict, with various resolutions emphasizing the importance of negotiations. However, the legal status of the territory remains contested. Morocco maintains that its sovereignty is justified under the principles of territorial integrity, which assert that colonial territories should not be fragmented without the consent of the administering power. This perspective aligns with Morocco's assertion that the Sahrawi people are part of the broader Moroccan nation, sharing a common history and cultural heritage.

The socio-economic benefits of integrating Western Sahara with Morocco are evident in the development projects and infrastructure investments that Morocco has initiated in the region. Over the years, Moroccan governance has led to significant improvements in local infrastructure, including roads, schools, and healthcare facilities, which have positively impacted the daily lives of Sahrawis. The enhanced connectivity between Western Sahara and the rest of Morocco promotes economic opportunities and social development, fostering a sense of unity and shared prosperity. This economic integration is crucial not only for the Sahrawi population but also for the stability of the entire region.

Cultural and linguistic ties between Sahrawis and Moroccans further reinforce the argument for integration. The majority of Sahrawis share a common language, Arabic, and cultural practices with other Moroccan communities, fostering a sense of belonging and mutual identity. The shared religious values, predominantly Islam, create a strong social bond that transcends regional differences. This cultural cohesion is vital for promoting social harmony and cooperation, ensuring that the diverse identities within Morocco are celebrated and integrated into a unified national narrative.

Finally, the implications of Moroccan governance on human rights and local governance are critical in understanding the broader context of sovereignty. Morocco's approach to human rights has evolved, with ongoing efforts to enhance local governance through the establishment of regional councils that empower local populations. This shift towards decentralization aims to ensure that the voices of Sahrawis are heard and their rights respected. Furthermore, the emphasis on environmental management and resource sharing highlights Morocco's commitment to sustainable development in Western Sahara. By fostering tourism and international recognition of Moroccan culture, the integration of Western Sahara not only enhances regional stability but also showcases the rich cultural tapestry that defines this unique part of the world.

Historical Claims of Morocco

The historical claims of Morocco regarding Western Sahara are rooted in a complex narrative that spans centuries, intertwining issues of territorial integrity, cultural identity, and geopolitical interests. Historically, the region has been an integral part of Moroccan territory, particularly during the era of the Moroccan Empire, which extended its influence across vast areas of North Africa. The historical maps and documentation from periods such as the 16th and 17th centuries illustrate Morocco's claim to the territory, with various dynasties exercising control over the land that is now Western Sahara. This historical context is crucial for understanding the contemporary claims and the rationale behind Morocco's position on the territorial dispute.

Moreover, the decolonization process in Africa has shaped the political landscape, leading to disputes over territorial claims. Following Spain's withdrawal from Western Sahara in 1975, Morocco asserted its historical rights over the territory, citing both legal and historical precedents. This assertion was bolstered by the Madrid Accords, which recognized Moroccan administrative control over the region. The argument for integration with Morocco is often framed within the context of preserving historical ties and the legitimacy of claims based on historical governance and cultural continuity. This perspective emphasizes the need for a resolution that acknowledges Morocco's historical connections to Western Sahara.

The cultural and linguistic ties between the Sahrawi people and Moroccans further strengthen the case for integration. Shared language, customs, and traditions create a common cultural fabric that binds the two groups. The Sahrawis, while maintaining their unique identity, have historically interacted with various Moroccan communities, resulting in a rich tapestry of cultural exchange. This interconnectedness is evident in shared practices, festivals, and social norms, which highlight the potential for a harmonious coexistence

9

within a united Moroccan state. The recognition of these cultural ties can foster a sense of belonging and community among the Sahrawis, thereby enhancing the argument for integration.

In addition to cultural considerations, the economic benefits of integration with Morocco present a compelling case for the future of Western Sahara. Morocco has invested significantly in infrastructure development and economic projects in the region, aiming to improve living standards and stimulate local economies. The establishment of trade routes, transportation networks, and access to markets facilitates economic growth and offers opportunities for job creation. This integration can lead to enhanced access to resources and investment, ultimately benefiting the Sahrawi population. The potential for economic development under Moroccan governance underscores the practical advantages that accompany historical claims.

Finally, the geopolitical stability of the region is a critical factor in the discussion of Western Sahara's future. Morocco's governance is often seen as a stabilizing force in a region marked by conflict and uncertainty. By promoting security and development, Morocco can address concerns regarding human rights and local governance, fostering an environment conducive to progress. The Moroccan approach to governance includes efforts to improve infrastructure, enhance resource management, and promote tourism, which can lead to international recognition of Moroccan culture in Western Sahara. This multifaceted strategy not only emphasizes Morocco's historical claims but also highlights the potential for a prosperous and unified future for the region.

Chapter 3: Economic Benefits of Integration with Morocco

Economic growth potential in Western Sahara, as part of Morocco, can be significantly enhanced through various avenues that leverage the region's rich resources and strategic location. The integration with Morocco offers a robust framework for economic development, primarily due to the opportunities presented by infrastructure investments, access to broader markets, and the pooling of resources. By aligning with Morocco's economic policies and development strategies, Western Sahara can benefit from increased trade, tourism, and investment, which are essential for fostering a sustainable and self-reliant economy.

Key to realizing this growth potential is the commitment of the Moroccan government to invest in infrastructure projects throughout Western Sahara. These projects include the development of roads, ports, and energy facilities that are crucial for connecting remote areas to major urban centers and facilitating trade. Improved infrastructure not only boosts local businesses by enhancing their operational capacities but also attracts foreign investment, which is vital for job creation and economic diversification. The establishment of a more integrated transportation network can also position Western Sahara as a logistical hub, further stimulating economic activities.

Moreover, the economic benefits of integration extend beyond infrastructure. The shared cultural and linguistic ties between Sahrawis and Moroccans can foster a cohesive business environment that encourages entrepreneurship and innovation. By promoting local craftsmanship, agriculture, and fisheries, the region can capitalize on its unique cultural heritage while enhancing the economic footprint of its communities. This cultural synergy can also attract tourism, which is a growing sector that can provide significant revenue streams and create employment opportunities for local populations.

The Moroccan governance model offers a framework for regional security and stability, which are critical components for economic development. A stable political environment encourages both domestic and foreign investments, as businesses are more likely to thrive in secure areas. The Moroccan government's emphasis on human rights and local governance further enhances this stability, reassuring investors and residents alike. By working together to address regional challenges, such as unemployment and resource management, both Moroccans and Sahrawis can contribute to a more prosperous and resilient economy.

Lastly, the international diplomatic support for Moroccan sovereignty provides an additional layer of economic assurance. Recognition from global powers can lead to favorable trade agreements and investment opportunities, positioning Western Sahara as an integral part of Morocco in the eyes of the international community. The potential for resource sharing and environmental management can also be optimized, ensuring sustainable development that respects the needs of the local population. Collectively, these factors underscore the significant economic growth potential that exists when Western Sahara remains integrated with Morocco, creating a pathway toward a prosperous future for its inhabitants.

Job Creation and Employment Opportunities

Job creation and employment opportunities are critical factors in the ongoing discourse surrounding Western Sahara's integration with Morocco. The integration promises to unlock significant economic potential, which in turn can lead to the establishment of various industries and services that can absorb the local workforce. With Morocco's diverse economy, which includes sectors such as agriculture, fisheries, mining, and tourism, the incorporation of Western Sahara into this framework can catalyze job creation. By fostering new business ventures and attracting investment, the region can witness a decrease in unemployment and an increase in overall living standards.

Moreover, the historical claims and territorial integrity associated with Moroccan governance can provide a stable backdrop for economic development. Stability is a crucial element for attracting both domestic and foreign investment. Investors are more likely to commit resources to areas that show a commitment to stability and growth. By becoming an integral part of Morocco, Western Sahara can benefit from the established legal frameworks and business environments that Morocco has developed, leading to enhanced job opportunities for its residents.

Additionally, the cultural and linguistic ties between Sahrawis and Moroccans can facilitate workforce integration and collaboration. Shared values and communication can promote a harmonious working environment, enhancing productivity and innovation. The existing cultural connections may also encourage businesses to engage local talent, ensuring that employment opportunities are accessible to Sahrawis. This not only boosts the local economy but also strengthens community ties, fostering a sense of unity that is essential for sustainable development.

Development projects and infrastructure investments by Morocco are already underway and have the potential to create numerous jobs in various sectors. The government's commitment to enhancing infrastructure such as roads, ports, and utilities will not only facilitate local businesses but also attract new enterprises. As infrastructure improves, opportunities in construction, maintenance, and service industries will emerge, providing immediate job prospects while laying the groundwork for long-term economic stability.

Finally, the international diplomatic support for Moroccan sovereignty can further enhance job creation and employment opportunities in Western Sahara. As Morocco strengthens its position on the global stage, the region may benefit from increased foreign investment and trade partnerships. This influx of resources can lead to diversified job markets and enhanced economic resilience. The focus on human rights and local governance under Moroccan administration can also ensure that employment practices are equitable, fostering an environment where all residents of Western Sahara can thrive within a broader Moroccan economy.

Infrastructure Development

Infrastructure development in Western Sahara is a pivotal aspect of the argument for its integration with Morocco. Over the years, Morocco has undertaken significant initiatives to enhance the region's infrastructure, which is essential for fostering economic growth, improving living standards, and ensuring regional stability. By investing in roads, ports, and telecommunications, Morocco not only facilitates better connectivity within Western Sahara but also strengthens its ties with the broader Moroccan economy. This integration is crucial for the development of a cohesive national identity, which is increasingly important in a region marked by diverse cultures and historical claims.

The historical context of infrastructure development in Western Sahara reveals a narrative of neglect under previous administrations. Morocco's commitment to infrastructure projects stands in stark contrast to the limited investment made during the period of conflict. The establishment of modern transportation networks and public services has the potential to transform the socioeconomic landscape of the region. As these projects progress, they create jobs, stimulate local economies, and provide essential services, making a compelling case for the benefits of remaining part of Morocco.

Economically, the integration of Western Sahara with Morocco presents numerous advantages. Morocco's strategic investments in infrastructure have the potential to unlock the region's resources, such as fisheries and phosphates, which are critical to both local and national economies. Improved infrastructure not only facilitates domestic trade but also enhances the potential for international trade, positioning Western Sahara as a vital link in Morocco's economic expansion. This integration is expected to attract foreign investment, leading to further economic development and diversification in the region.

Culturally and linguistically, the ties between Sahrawis and Moroccans are reinforced through shared infrastructure projects. These initiatives often involve collaboration and participation from local communities, fostering a sense of unity and common purpose. As Moroccans and Sahrawis work together on development projects, cultural exchange becomes inevitable, enhancing mutual understanding and respect. This cultural synergy is vital for promoting social cohesion, which is essential in a region where diverse identities coexist.

Finally, the role of infrastructure development in ensuring security and stability in Western Sahara cannot be overlooked. By establishing a robust infrastructure network, Morocco enhances its governance capabilities in the region, allowing for better law enforcement and public safety measures. This stability attracts tourism and enhances the international recognition of Moroccan culture in Western Sahara. Moreover, a well-developed infrastructure supports environmental management and resource sharing, ensuring sustainable use of the region's natural assets. In this context, infrastructure development is not merely a matter of economic growth but a fundamental component of fostering a stable and prosperous future for Western Sahara within the framework of Moroccan sovereignty.

Chapter 4: Cultural and Linguistic Ties Between Sahrawis and Moroccans

The concept of shared linguistic heritage serves as a vital link between the Sahrawi population and Morocco, reinforcing the argument for Western Sahara's integration with the Moroccan state. Arabic, as the primary language of both Moroccans and Sahrawis, fosters a sense of belonging and cultural continuity. This linguistic connection transcends mere communication; it embodies shared histories, traditions, and values that have evolved over centuries. In a region marked by diverse influences, the Arabic language acts as a unifying force, enabling the inhabitants of Western Sahara to connect with Moroccan culture and identity.

Historically, the Sahrawi people have been influenced by the Arabic-speaking communities that have thrived in the region for generations. The spread of the Arabic language, alongside the teachings of Islam, has woven a complex tapestry of cultural interactions that shape the identity of both Sahrawis and Moroccans. The historical significance of this linguistic bond cannot be understated; it reflects centuries of coexistence and mutual influence. As such, the integration with Morocco is not merely a political maneuver but a continuation of a long-established relationship founded on shared heritage.

The economic implications of this shared linguistic and cultural heritage further bolster the case for integration. A common language facilitates trade, commerce, and economic collaboration, opening avenues for Sahrawis to access Moroccan markets and resources. The linguistic ties enable better communication and understanding among various economic stakeholders, promoting investment and development initiatives in Western Sahara. This economic synergy is crucial for the region's growth, providing opportunities for local communities to thrive within the larger Moroccan economy.

Furthermore, the cultural and linguistic ties between Sahrawis and Moroccans extend to shared religious and social values. Islam, which is predominant in both communities, enriches the social fabric and reinforces a sense of unity. Religious practices and traditions are often similar, fostering a collective identity that transcends regional differences. This shared framework not only contributes to social cohesion but also enhances the potential for collaborative governance and community engagement under Moroccan administration.

In conclusion, the shared linguistic heritage between Sahrawis and Moroccans is a cornerstone of the argument for Western Sahara's integration with Morocco. This bond strengthens historical claims and territorial integrity while presenting significant economic advantages. As both communities continue to navigate their identities in a changing world, the recognition of their shared language and culture will be pivotal in fostering stability and promoting development in the region.

Cultural Practices and Traditions

Cultural practices and traditions in Western Sahara are deeply intertwined with those of Morocco, reflecting a rich tapestry of shared heritage that dates back centuries. The Sahrawi people, primarily of Arab-Berber descent, have a cultural identity that resonates strongly with Moroccan traditions. This connection is evident in various aspects of daily life, including music, dance, and culinary practices. Traditional Sahrawi music, characterized by its rhythmic beats and poetic lyrics, often mirrors Moroccan styles, fostering a sense of unity through artistic expression. Moreover, festivals and communal gatherings highlight the blending of cultural elements, showcasing a vibrant celebration of identity that spans both regions.

The linguistic ties between the Sahrawis and Moroccans further illustrate the cultural connection. Arabic, particularly the Hassaniya dialect spoken in Western Sahara, serves as a linguistic bridge that facilitates communication and cultural exchange. This shared language not only enhances interpersonal relationships but also strengthens the collective identity of the Sahrawi people within the broader Moroccan context. The preservation of language and dialect plays a crucial role in maintaining cultural heritage, ensuring that traditions are passed down through generations. Consequently, linguistic ties foster a sense of belonging and reinforce the argument for Western Sahara's integration with Morocco.

Religious practices also form a significant aspect of the cultural fabric shared between Western Sahara and Morocco. The predominant faith in both regions is Islam, which influences social norms, ethical values, and communal activities. Religious celebrations, such as Eid al-Fitr and Eid al-Adha, are observed with much enthusiasm in both cultures, reflecting shared beliefs and practices. The role of religious leaders and institutions further solidifies this connection, as they often serve as mediators in community matters and promote social cohesion. This common religious foundation supports the notion that cultural affinity can enhance the stability and harmony within a unified Moroccan state.

Moreover, traditional crafts and artisanal skills exemplify the cultural interconnections between the two regions. Sahrawi artisans, known for their intricate handicrafts, often draw inspiration from Moroccan designs, creating products that are not only culturally significant but also economically viable. The promotion of traditional crafts can boost local economies through tourism and trade, providing a sustainable source of income for communities in Western Sahara. By integrating these cultural practices into the broader Moroccan economy, the potential for growth and development is significantly enhanced, benefiting both the Sahrawis and the Moroccan state.

In conclusion, the cultural practices and traditions of Western Sahara and Morocco form a strong foundation for advocating integration. The shared linguistic, religious, and artistic elements illustrate a profound connection that transcends political boundaries. By embracing these cultural ties, both regions stand to gain economically and socially, fostering a sense of unity that is essential for regional stability. The recognition of this shared cultural heritage not only bolsters the case for Western Sahara's integration with Morocco but also highlights the potential for a harmonious future built on mutual respect and understanding.

Chapter 5: Security and stability in the region under Moroccan governance

Enhancements in regional security are a critical consideration in the ongoing discourse regarding Western Sahara's integration with Morocco. The region has faced numerous challenges, including territorial disputes and the potential for conflict. By integrating with Morocco, Western Sahara can benefit from a more robust security framework that has the potential to ensure stability and peace for its inhabitants. Moroccan governance has historically played a significant role in maintaining order and addressing security concerns, which would be essential for the continued peace and safety of both Moroccan citizens and the Sahrawi population.

Under Moroccan governance, the region would likely see an increase in coordinated security efforts aimed at combating threats such as terrorism and organized crime. Morocco has a well-established security apparatus and a history of successful counter-terrorism operations. By incorporating Western Sahara into this framework, there would be an enhanced capability to respond to security threats, ensuring a safer environment for all residents. This would not only protect local citizens but also enhance Morocco's position as a stable ally in the broader North African region.

Moreover, the integration of Western Sahara with Morocco would facilitate more effective intelligence sharing and collaboration among regional security forces. This kind of cooperation is vital in addressing transnational issues that affect the stability of the entire region. With shared resources and strategic planning, both Moroccan and Sahrawi populations could benefit from a collective approach to security that would deter potential aggressors and foster a sense of unity among diverse communities. The resulting synergy would contribute to a more secure and resilient region.

In addition to direct security enhancements, the integration could lead to improved socio-economic conditions, further bolstering stability. Morocco has demonstrated a commitment to developing the region through infrastructure projects and economic initiatives, which would create jobs and promote social cohesion. Economic stability often correlates with enhanced security, as communities with better economic prospects are less likely to fall into conflict. The Moroccan government's focus on development would thus play a crucial role in alleviating grievances and promoting peace.

Ultimately, the prospect of enhanced regional security under Moroccan governance is intertwined with broader themes of cooperation, development, and unity. The integration of Western Sahara into Morocco not only promises to mitigate existing tensions but also sets a foundation for a collaborative future. By prioritizing security and stability, both the Moroccan state and the Sahrawi people can work together towards a more peaceful and prosperous coexistence, aligning their interests and fostering a sense of shared identity that transcends historical divisions.

Countering extremism and instability

C ountering extremism and instability in the context of Western Sahara's integration with Morocco is crucial for ensuring a peaceful and prosperous future for the region. As the world grapples with the rise of extremist ideologies, the need for a stable and unified governance model becomes increasingly clear. Morocco's approach to integrating Western Sahara not only addresses the historical claims and territorial integrity but also promotes a framework that can effectively counter potential threats. By fostering a sense of belonging and identity within the larger Moroccan state, the integration process can help mitigate feelings of disenfranchisement that often fuel extremism.

The historical ties between the Sahrawi people and Morocco provide a foundation for stability. These connections, rooted in shared history and cultural narratives, can serve as a bulwark against radical influences. By emphasizing these bonds, Moroccan governance can cultivate a collective identity that transcends tribal and regional divisions. This unity is essential in creating a resilient society capable of resisting extremist ideologies that thrive on division and discord. A cohesive national identity not only strengthens social fabric but also enhances the legitimacy of governance structures in the eyes of the local population.

Economically, the integration of Western Sahara with Morocco presents numerous benefits that can contribute to long-term stability. Through infrastructure investments and development projects, Morocco has the potential to significantly improve living standards in the region. Economic opportunities will not only alleviate poverty but also provide alternatives to radicalization. As local communities witness tangible benefits from their integration into the Moroccan state, they are more likely to embrace stability and reject extremist narratives that offer no productive path forward. This economic upliftment can thus act as a deterrent against instability.

Security considerations are paramount in the region, given the complex geopolitical landscape. Morocco has established itself as a key player in promoting regional security through its counter-terrorism efforts and collaborations with international partners. By integrating Western Sahara, Morocco can extend its security framework to cover this area comprehensively, addressing potential vulnerabilities. This proactive stance not only enhances safety within Western Sahara but also contributes to a more stable North African region, reducing the risks posed by extremist groups that may seek to exploit instability for their own agendas.

Lastly, the cultural and social values shared between the Sahrawis and Moroccans play a significant role in countering extremism. The common religious beliefs, social practices, and community structures foster a sense of solidarity that can effectively counter radical influences. By promoting these shared values, Moroccan governance can create a narrative that emphasizes coexistence and mutual respect. This cultural integration is essential in building a resilient society that values diversity while finding strength in unity, thereby thwarting attempts by extremist elements to sow discord and division within the region.

Chapter 6: Development projects and infrastructure investments by Morocco

The integration of Western Sahara with Morocco holds significant potential for the development of critical infrastructure projects that can enhance the region's economic landscape and improve the quality of life for its inhabitants. Morocco has embarked on various initiatives aimed at expanding transportation networks, energy supply, and communication systems in Western Sahara. These projects not only facilitate the movement of goods and people but also promote regional connectivity, aligning Western Sahara's development with broader national goals. By investing in roads, railways, and ports, Morocco aims to establish Western Sahara as a vital economic corridor that will foster trade and investment opportunities.

One of the cornerstone infrastructure projects is the enhancement of the road network connecting Western Sahara to major Moroccan cities. Upgrading existing roads and constructing new ones will significantly reduce travel times and increase access to markets, healthcare, and education. This improved connectivity will benefit local businesses and create jobs, contributing to economic stability in the region. Additionally, the development of logistics hubs and transport services can attract investments from various sectors, stimulating growth and diversification of the local economy.

Energy projects also play a pivotal role in the integration process. Morocco has made substantial strides in renewable energy, particularly in solar and wind power. By extending these projects into Western Sahara, the region can harness its natural resources to produce clean energy, reduce dependence on fossil fuels, and promote sustainability. This transition not only aligns with global environmental goals but also provides opportunities for local communities to engage in green jobs and entrepreneurship, fostering a sense of ownership and participation in the region's development.

The importance of communication infrastructure cannot be understated in the context of modernization and integration. Morocco has prioritized the expansion of digital connectivity in Western Sahara, working to improve internet access and telecommunications. With enhanced connectivity, residents can access information, education, and services more readily, bridging the gap between urban and rural areas. This digital transformation is essential for empowering local populations, fostering innovation, and integrating Western Sahara into the global economy.

Overall, the key infrastructure projects initiated by Morocco in Western Sahara reflect a commitment to fostering economic growth, improving living standards, and promoting stability in the region. By prioritizing investments in transportation, energy, and communication, Morocco not only enhances the prospects for Western Sahara's development but also reinforces the historical and cultural ties that bind the region to the Moroccan state. The success of these initiatives will ultimately demonstrate the mutual benefits of integration and pave the way for a prosperous future for all inhabitants of the region.

Impact on Local Communities

The integration of Western Sahara with Morocco has profound implications for local communities, particularly in terms of economic, social, and cultural dynamics. One of the most significant impacts is the potential for economic development through enhanced investment and infrastructure projects. Morocco has demonstrated a commitment to improving the living conditions in Western Sahara, with initiatives aimed at boosting local economies through job creation, better healthcare, and education. The integration allows for the sharing of resources that can lead to improved public services, which are crucial for the development of local communities that have historically faced challenges due to isolation and limited access to opportunities.

Culturally, the ties between Sahrawis and Moroccans are deeply rooted in shared history, language, and traditions. This cultural affinity fosters a sense of belonging and unity, which can be pivotal in creating a cohesive society. By being part of Morocco, Western Sahara can benefit from enhanced cultural exchange, allowing for the preservation and promotion of local customs while integrating them into the broader Moroccan identity. This cultural integration can empower local communities by recognizing their unique heritage while providing a platform for cultural expression and collaboration.

Security and stability are paramount concerns for local communities, especially in regions that have experienced conflict. Moroccan governance is often viewed as a stabilizing force, contributing to enhanced security in Western Sahara. This stability can lead to a safer environment for families and businesses, encouraging investment and community engagement. Moreover, the Moroccan state's commitment to human rights and local governance can create an atmosphere where community voices are heard, fostering a sense of ownership and responsibility among residents regarding their governance.

The environmental management and resource-sharing initiatives under Moroccan governance are also critical in supporting local communities. Morocco is known for its efforts in sustainable development, and integrating Western Sahara into this framework can help address environmental challenges unique to the region. Through collaborative efforts, local communities can benefit from resource management practices that ensure the responsible use of natural resources, promoting both environmental sustainability and economic resilience.

Finally, the potential for tourism and international recognition of Moroccan culture in Western Sahara can significantly impact local communities. By promoting the region as a tourist destination, local economies can flourish, providing new avenues for income and employment. The cultural richness of Western Sahara, combined with its strategic location, positions it as an attractive destination for both domestic and international tourists. This influx not only boosts the economy but also fosters a greater appreciation for the diverse cultural landscape of Morocco, ultimately enhancing the identity and pride of local communities.

Chapter 7: International Diplomatic Support for Moroccan Sovereignty

Recognition by global powers plays a crucial role in shaping the geopolitical landscape of Western Sahara and its integration with Morocco. The international community's acknowledgment of Morocco's sovereignty over Western Sahara significantly influences regional stability, economic development, and the overall prosperity of the area. Countries that recognize Morocco's claims contribute to a framework of legitimacy, which not only strengthens Morocco's position but also encourages investment and cooperation in the region. This recognition is essential for fostering a sense of unity and purpose among the diverse populations of Western Sahara and Morocco.

Historically, the ties between Western Sahara and Morocco are deeply rooted, with claims based on a shared heritage that spans centuries. The historical context reveals that the Sahrawi people have longstanding connections to Moroccan culture and governance. These ties underscore the argument for integration, as they highlight the natural alignment of interests and identities that has persisted through various political changes. The integration of Western Sahara with Morocco is not merely a contemporary issue; it is part of a historical continuum that reflects a collective identity and destiny.

The economic benefits of integrating Western Sahara with Morocco are substantial. Morocco has already initiated various development projects and infrastructure investments in the region, aimed at improving living standards and fostering economic growth. These initiatives have generated employment opportunities, enhanced access to education and healthcare, and facilitated trade. The potential for economic synergy is immense, as the integration can lead to a more robust market and better resource management, ultimately benefiting both the Sahrawis and Moroccans. A united economic front can attract further investment from global powers seeking stability and potential in the region.

Cultural and linguistic ties between the Sahrawis and Moroccans further support the case for integration. The shared language, traditions, and social practices create a rich tapestry of cultural identity that transcends political boundaries. This cultural unity fosters mutual respect and understanding, reinforcing the idea that integration can enhance rather than diminish local identities. Additionally, shared religious values contribute to a sense of community and belonging, which is fundamental in promoting regional cohesion and social harmony.

Finally, the security and stability in the region under Moroccan governance are crucial for maintaining peace and preventing conflicts. Morocco's commitment to human rights and local governance is also vital, as it assures the Sahrawi population of their rights and participation in the political process. Effective environmental management and resource sharing are essential for sustainable development, ensuring that both communities benefit from their natural resources. The promotion of tourism and international recognition of Moroccan culture in Western Sahara can further enhance the region's profile on the global stage, solidifying the case for integration and fostering a sense of pride among its inhabitants.

Role of the United Nations

The role of the United Nations in the context of Western Sahara has been pivotal since the region's decolonization process began in the mid-20th century. The UN's involvement stems from its mandate to promote peace and stability globally, particularly in areas with unresolved territorial disputes. In the case of Western Sahara, the UN has facilitated discussions and negotiations between Morocco and the Sahrawi nationalist movement, known as the Polisario Front. This engagement aims to find a mutually acceptable solution to the conflict, emphasizing the importance of self-determination and the principle of territorial integrity for Morocco. However, the complexities of the situation have led to a prolonged stalemate, highlighting the challenges faced by the UN in effectively mediating such disputes.

Historically, the UN has recognized Morocco's claims over Western Sahara, tracing back to the region's status as a Spanish colony. Following Spain's withdrawal in 1975, Morocco asserted its territorial claims, which has been a point of contention ever since. The UN's attempts to facilitate a referendum for self-determination have been hampered by various factors, including the differing interpretations of what self-determination entails and the lack of consensus on the electorate's composition. This historical context is essential to understanding the UN's role and the ongoing dialogue surrounding Western Sahara's status.

Economically, integration with Morocco presents significant benefits for the Sahrawi people. The UN has noted the potential for economic development in the region, emphasizing the importance of stability for attracting investment and fostering growth. Morocco's ongoing development projects in Western Sahara aim to improve infrastructure, create jobs, and enhance access to education and healthcare. These efforts have the potential to uplift the local economy, which has historically suffered from underdevelopment. The UN's advocacy for economic cooperation underscores the need for a collaborative approach to harness the region's resources for the benefit of all its inhabitants.

Culturally and linguistically, the ties between the Sahrawis and Moroccans are deeply rooted, further complicating the political landscape. The UN acknowledges the shared heritage, language, and religious practices that bind these communities. This cultural unity can serve as a foundation for fostering peace and reconciliation. The UN's support for dialogue and cultural exchange initiatives is vital in promoting understanding and cooperation between different groups within Western Sahara, ultimately contributing to a more harmonious society.

Lastly, the UN's role extends to monitoring human rights and governance in the region. While Morocco's governance has faced criticism, it has also implemented various reforms aimed at enhancing local governance and protecting human rights. The UN's presence in the area is crucial for ensuring that these rights are respected and for providing a platform for dialogue between the Moroccan authorities and the Sahrawi community. The interplay of governance, security, and human rights under Moroccan administration is a significant aspect of the UN's ongoing engagement in Western Sahara, reflecting its commitment to fostering a peaceful and prosperous future for all residents.

Chapter 8: Shared religious and social values

Islam has played a pivotal role in shaping the cultural, social, and political landscape of Western Sahara and Morocco. As a common foundation, Islam binds the people of these regions together, fostering a sense of unity and shared identity. The majority of the Sahrawi population adheres to Islam, which permeates their daily lives, values, and traditions. This shared faith not only influences social norms but also promotes a collective understanding of justice, community, and governance, aligning closely with the principles upheld by Moroccan society. In this context, Islam serves as a crucial element in advocating for the integration of Western Sahara with Morocco, highlighting the importance of spiritual and cultural unity.

The historical claims surrounding Western Sahara are deeply intertwined with Islamic heritage. The region has a long-standing Islamic history, characterized by the spread of Islam through trade and cultural exchange. Historical records indicate that the Sahrawis and Moroccans share ancestral ties that date back centuries, marked by the establishment of trade routes and intermarriages between the two communities. This shared history extends to the struggle against colonialism, where both groups fought to preserve their Islamic identity and territorial integrity. Recognizing this common heritage reinforces the argument for Western Sahara's integration with Morocco, as it emphasizes the continuity of Islamic values and traditions that have long been upheld by both peoples.

Economic cooperation between Morocco and Western Sahara underlines the benefits of integration, further supported by Islamic principles of mutual assistance and prosperity. Morocco has committed to significant investments in the region, aimed at developing infrastructure, enhancing local economies, and creating job opportunities. This economic support is built upon the Islamic ethos of fostering community welfare and ensuring that resources are shared equitably. By integrating with Morocco, Western Sahara stands to gain from improved access to markets, increased tourism, and the potential for sustainable development initiatives. Such economic integration not only aligns with the Islamic principle of promoting the common good but also enhances the quality of life for Sahrawis.

Culturally and linguistically, the ties between Sahrawis and Moroccans are robust, further solidifying Islam as a common foundation. The Arabic language, which is deeply rooted in Islamic tradition, serves as a primary means of communication for both groups. This shared linguistic heritage facilitates cultural exchange and strengthens community bonds. Moreover, Islamic festivals, traditions, and rituals are celebrated across both regions, reinforcing a collective identity. By embracing their shared cultural and linguistic ties, the Sahrawi people can enjoy a richer cultural experience under Moroccan governance, which honors and promotes these traditions.

The integration of Western Sahara with Morocco also holds significant implications for security and stability in the region. The shared Islamic values promote peace, tolerance, and social cohesion, which are essential for maintaining order in a diverse society. Moroccan governance has demonstrated a commitment to enhancing security through various development projects and infrastructure investments that contribute to regional stability. Additionally, the international diplomatic support for Moroccan sovereignty reinforces an environment conducive to peace and cooperation. By uniting under a common Islamic foundation, both Moroccans and Sahrawis can work towards a harmonious future, ensuring that their shared values lead to a prosperous and stable region.

Social cohesion and community bonds

The integration of Western Sahara with Morocco has significant implications for social cohesion and community bonds within the region. Historically, the Sahrawi people have shared numerous cultural, linguistic, and religious ties with Moroccans, fostering a sense of belonging that transcends arbitrary political borders. This interconnectedness is rooted in centuries of shared history, traditions, and social practices, which have created a foundation for mutual understanding and cooperation. Strengthening these bonds through formal integration can enhance social unity and foster a collective identity, allowing communities to thrive together rather than in isolation.

Economic integration between Western Sahara and Morocco presents an opportunity for enhanced social cohesion through improved living conditions and shared prosperity. By aligning Western Sahara's economic development with Morocco's broader economic strategies, both regions can benefit from increased investment, job creation, and infrastructure development. These economic benefits not only improve the quality of life for the Sahrawi people but also encourage social interactions and interdependence between communities. As local economies grow, the potential for collaborative projects and partnerships increases, reinforcing community ties and creating a shared vision for progress.

The concept of territorial integrity plays a crucial role in fostering social cohesion. The unification of Western Sahara with Morocco can mitigate the fragmentation that arises from prolonged disputes and territorial claims. By establishing a stable governance framework under Moroccan authority, communities can focus on collaboration rather than division. This unity can lead to the development of policies that prioritize local needs and enhance community participation in governance, thus reinforcing the bonds among residents. A shared governance structure can empower the Sahrawi population, allowing them to contribute to decision-making processes and fostering a sense of ownership over their future.

Cultural exchange and mutual respect are essential elements in building robust community bonds. The rich cultural tapestry of Morocco, encompassing various traditions, languages, and practices, can serve as a unifying force for Sahrawis. Integration with Morocco can promote the preservation and celebration of Sahrawi culture while simultaneously introducing diverse Moroccan cultural elements that enrich the local community. This cultural synergy can foster a sense of pride among residents, encouraging them to embrace their heritage while also participating in a broader national identity that values diversity as a strength.

Lastly, the promotion of stability and security under Moroccan governance can significantly enhance social cohesion and community bonds. A stable environment allows individuals and families to engage in social, economic, and cultural activities without the fear of conflict or instability. As security is prioritized, communities can focus on building relationships, supporting one another, and working together toward common goals. In this context, the integration of Western Sahara with Morocco not only promises to protect the region's territorial integrity but also to cultivate a resilient social fabric that values unity in diversity, ultimately benefiting all citizens involved.

Chapter 9: Impact of Moroccan governance on human rights and local governance

Human rights improvements in Western Sahara have become a focal point in discussions about its integration with Morocco. The historical context of the region, characterized by prolonged conflict and political struggles, has often overshadowed the potential for progress in human rights. Since Morocco assumed control over the territory, there have been significant strides made in enhancing the rights and freedoms of the Sahrawi people. These improvements are not merely coincidental; they stem from Morocco's commitment to integrating Western Sahara into its broader national framework, which emphasizes the importance of human rights as a cornerstone of governance.

Under Moroccan administration, various initiatives have been launched to promote human rights standards in Western Sahara. Morocco has adopted a series of reforms aimed at improving the living conditions of Sahrawis, including investments in education and healthcare. These efforts have resulted in increased access to essential services, which are crucial for the development of human capital in the region. Furthermore, the establishment of local governance structures has empowered Sahrawis to participate actively in decision-making processes, thereby enhancing their political rights and representation.

The Moroccan government has also made strides in addressing issues of civil and political liberties. By fostering an environment where freedom of expression and assembly are respected, Sahrawis have been able to voice their concerns and advocate for their rights more effectively. Human rights organizations operating in the region have noted improvements in the treatment of detainees and the reduction of arbitrary arrests. Such developments are indicative of Morocco's broader commitment to uphold the rule of law and protect individual rights within its territorial boundaries.

Economic integration with Morocco has further contributed to human rights advancements in Western Sahara. Increased investments and development projects have not only boosted the local economy but have also created job opportunities, allowing Sahrawis to improve their livelihoods. With economic stability comes the potential for enhanced social rights, as communities become more resilient and better positioned to demand their rights. The positive correlation between economic development and human rights underscores the importance of a unified approach to governance that prioritizes the welfare of all citizens.

International diplomatic support for Morocco's sovereignty over Western Sahara has also played a crucial role in fostering an environment conducive to human rights improvements. As Morocco strengthens its international standing, it is held accountable for its human rights record, leading to further reforms and adherence to international standards. This support, paired with shared cultural and social values between Moroccans and Sahrawis, creates a solid foundation for ongoing progress in human rights. As the integration of Western Sahara with Morocco continues, the focus on human rights will remain integral to ensuring that all citizens can enjoy the benefits of a stable, prosperous society.

Local governance structures

Local governance structures in Western Sahara play a crucial role in the integration of the region with Morocco. The existing administrative framework reflects a blend of traditional Sahrawi leadership and Moroccan administrative practices. This hybrid governance system fosters local participation and aligns with Morocco's broader national policies, ensuring that the voices of the Sahrawi population are represented within the Moroccan state. The integration of local governance structures into the Moroccan administrative system can enhance political stability and foster a sense of community among the diverse populations living in the region.

Historically, the governance of Western Sahara has been influenced by both Sahrawi traditions and Moroccan practices, leading to a unique governance model. The region has traditionally been characterized by tribal leadership and communal decision-making processes, which coexist with the formal structures established by Moroccan authorities. This duality allows for the preservation of cultural identity while promoting a unified state structure. As Morocco emphasizes its historical claims over the territory, the integration of local governance structures can help reinforce the legitimacy of Moroccan sovereignty in Western Sahara.

Economically, the integration of Western Sahara into Morocco presents numerous benefits facilitated by effective local governance. The Moroccan government has invested heavily in the region, targeting infrastructure development, job creation, and resource management. Local governance structures can play a vital role in ensuring that these investments are aligned with the needs of the Sahrawi population, fostering economic growth and stability. Furthermore, the collaboration between local authorities and Moroccan institutions can enhance the capacity for sustainable development and effective resource sharing, benefiting both the local community and the Moroccan state.

Culturally and linguistically, the ties between Sahrawis and Moroccans form an essential foundation for successful governance. The shared language and cultural practices foster social cohesion and mutual understanding, which are critical for effective governance. Local governance structures can help to preserve and promote Sahrawi culture while integrating it within the broader Moroccan context. This cultural synergy not only supports the regional identity of Western Sahara but also strengthens the collective Moroccan identity, reinforcing the notion of unity in diversity.

Finally, the security and stability of the region are paramount under Moroccan governance. The Moroccan government has prioritized the establishment of a safe and secure environment in Western Sahara, which is crucial for attracting investment and promoting tourism. Local governance structures are key to addressing security concerns at the community level and ensuring that local populations feel both protected and involved in governance processes. By fostering collaboration between local leaders and Moroccan authorities, the governance model in Western Sahara can contribute to the region's overall stability, enhancing human rights and development prospects for its residents.

Chapter 10: Environmental management and resource sharing

Sustainable resource management in Western Sahara is crucial for fostering economic growth and ensuring the long-term viability of the region's natural assets. As part of Morocco, Western Sahara can benefit from a more coordinated approach to resource allocation and environmental stewardship. Morocco has a proven track record of implementing sustainable practices in various sectors, including agriculture, fisheries, and renewable energy. By integrating Western Sahara into this framework, the region can leverage Morocco's experience and resources to develop sustainable practices that respect the environment while promoting economic development.

The diverse natural resources found in Western Sahara, including phosphates, fisheries, and renewable energy potential, require careful management to prevent exploitation and degradation. Morocco's commitment to sustainable development can help establish a regulatory framework that prioritizes environmental conservation and responsible resource utilization. This approach not only protects the region's ecosystems but also ensures that local communities benefit from the sustainable use of these resources, fostering economic resilience and social equity.

Cultural and linguistic ties between the Sahrawis and Moroccans can enhance cooperation in sustainable resource management. Both groups share common values and traditions that emphasize the importance of stewardship over natural resources. By promoting collaborative decision-making processes that involve local communities, Moroccan governance can ensure that the voices of Sahrawis are heard and respected. This participatory approach can lead to more effective management strategies that balance economic needs with environmental protection, ultimately fostering a sense of ownership and responsibility among the local population.

Investment in development projects and infrastructure by Morocco presents significant opportunities for sustainable resource management in Western Sahara. Infrastructure improvements can facilitate better access to markets, education, and healthcare, all of which are essential for promoting sustainable livelihoods. Furthermore, these investments can support the development of sectors such as ecotourism, which aligns with sustainable practices while generating economic benefits for local communities. By enhancing the region's infrastructure, Morocco can help create a more sustainable economic model that benefits both the Sahrawis and the broader Moroccan population.

Finally, international diplomatic support for Moroccan sovereignty reinforces the potential for sustainable resource management in Western Sahara. As Morocco continues to gain recognition on the global stage, it can attract foreign investment and partnerships focused on sustainable development initiatives. By aligning its strategies with international best practices and standards for resource management, Morocco can help ensure that Western Sahara's rich natural resources are utilized responsibly, ensuring long-term benefits for the region while maintaining environmental integrity. This collaborative, inclusive approach to resource management can serve as a model for addressing the challenges of sustainability in diverse contexts.

Collaborative environmental initiatives

Collaborative environmental initiatives play a crucial role in the discourse surrounding the integration of Western Sahara with Morocco. The region's unique ecosystem, characterized by arid landscapes and limited water resources, necessitates cooperative efforts to address environmental challenges. Both the Moroccan government and local Sahrawi communities can benefit from shared strategies aimed at sustainable resource management, which not only preserves the environment but also promotes economic development. Collaborative initiatives can lead to improved agricultural practices, better water management, and the protection of biodiversity, ultimately enhancing the quality of life for residents in the area.

One significant aspect of these collaborative initiatives is the promotion of sustainable fishing practices along the coast of Western Sahara. The rich marine resources in these waters are vital for the livelihoods of many Sahrawis. By integrating Moroccan policies with local fishing practices, there can be a balanced approach that ensures the preservation of fish stocks while supporting the local economy. This not only fosters collaboration between the Moroccan government and local fishermen but also encourages a sense of ownership and responsibility towards the marine environment, which is essential for long-term sustainability.

Furthermore, joint efforts in environmental education and awareness can strengthen the ties between Moroccan authorities and Sahrawi communities. Programs aimed at educating local populations about the importance of environmental conservation can empower individuals to engage in sustainable practices. Such initiatives can include workshops, community clean-up efforts, and the establishment of protected areas. By involving local residents in decision-making processes related to environmental management, these initiatives can build trust and foster a sense of unity, reinforcing the cultural and linguistic ties that bind Sahrawis and Moroccans.

Investment in renewable energy projects is another avenue for collaborative environmental initiatives. Morocco has made significant strides in harnessing solar and wind energy, and extending these efforts to Western Sahara can provide clean energy solutions for the region. Such projects not only contribute to environmental sustainability but also create job opportunities and stimulate economic growth. The development of renewable energy infrastructure can serve as a model for cooperation that transcends political boundaries, showcasing the potential benefits of integration and shared goals for a sustainable future.

Finally, international diplomatic support for Moroccan sovereignty can further enhance collaborative efforts in environmental management. As global awareness of climate change and environmental issues rises, the backing of international organizations can facilitate funding and resources for joint initiatives. This support can enable Morocco and Western Sahara to participate in broader environmental agreements and programs, reinforcing their commitment to sustainable development. Ultimately, through collaborative environmental initiatives, the integration of Western Sahara with Morocco can yield not only ecological benefits but also contribute to the region's stability and prosperity.

Chapter 11: Tourism and international recognition of Moroccan culture in Western Sahara

Cultural tourism in Western Sahara presents an opportunity to showcase the region's rich heritage and its deep connections with Moroccan culture. The diverse traditions, languages, and historical narratives of the Sahrawi people are intertwined with the broader Moroccan identity. By integrating with Morocco, Western Sahara can benefit from enhanced tourism infrastructure that promotes cultural exchange and appreciation. This integration will not only attract visitors interested in exploring the unique cultural landscape but also foster a greater understanding of the shared history that binds the Sahrawis and Moroccans.

The historical claims to the region further augment its tourism potential. Sites of historical significance, such as ancient caravan routes and indigenous settlements, tell the story of a land that has long been a crossroads of cultures. As Morocco continues to promote its rich historical narrative, Western Sahara can play a crucial role in this narrative, offering tourists a chance to engage with the complexities of its past. The promotion of historical tourism can lead to increased visitor numbers, benefiting local economies while simultaneously preserving and honoring the region's heritage.

Cultural and linguistic ties between Sahrawis and Moroccans are fundamental in shaping the tourism landscape. The shared Arabic language and common traditions such as music, dance, and cuisine create a seamless cultural experience for visitors. By fostering these connections, tourism can become a platform for dialogue and mutual understanding. Cultural festivals and events that celebrate both Sahrawi and Moroccan heritage can attract international attention, showcasing the region's diversity while reinforcing its integration with Morocco.

Security and stability under Moroccan governance are essential for the development of a thriving cultural tourism sector. A stable environment fosters confidence among tourists, encouraging them to explore the region. Moroccan governance provides a framework for ensuring safety and reliability, which are critical factors for potential visitors. With the support of local authorities, cultural tourism can flourish, leading to improved local governance and a more robust economy that benefits all residents of Western Sahara.

Development projects and infrastructure investments by Morocco will significantly enhance the cultural tourism potential of Western Sahara. Improved roads, facilities, and services will make the region more accessible to tourists. Additionally, investment in cultural sites and museums will help preserve local heritage while educating visitors about the unique stories of the Sahrawi people. As Morocco continues to promote its cultural assets, Western Sahara stands to gain from this integration, ensuring that its rich cultural tapestry is recognized and appreciated on both national and international stages.

Global recognition of Sahrawi culture

Global recognition of Sahrawi culture is an essential aspect of understanding the broader narrative surrounding Western Sahara and its integration with Morocco. The Sahrawi people, with their unique traditions, language, and social structures, have contributed significantly to the cultural tapestry of the region. Their rich oral history, music, and art reflect a vibrant identity that deserves acknowledgment on the global stage. However, this recognition is often overshadowed by political disputes, leading to a need for greater emphasis on Sahrawi culture as a vital component of Morocco's cultural heritage.

The historical claims to Western Sahara are deeply intertwined with Sahrawi culture. The region has served as a crossroads for various civilizations over centuries, influencing the development of local customs and traditions. The Sahrawis have historically inhabited this land, cultivating a distinct identity that encompasses their nomadic lifestyle, traditional crafts, and unique culinary practices. Recognition of this cultural heritage is crucial for fostering a sense of belonging and continuity among the Sahrawi people and strengthening their ties to the broader Moroccan identity.

Culturally and linguistically, there are significant ties between the Sahrawis and Moroccans, which provide a strong foundation for integration. The Arabic language serves as a unifying element, while shared customs and traditions create a sense of kinship. Festivals, music, and storytelling are common threads that bind these communities together. By embracing these cultural similarities, Morocco can promote a cohesive national identity that celebrates diversity while encouraging unity, ultimately enhancing social stability in the region.

Economic benefits associated with the integration of Western Sahara into Morocco can also contribute to the recognition and promotion of Sahrawi culture. Investment in infrastructure, tourism, and local industries can create opportunities for Sahrawis to showcase their cultural heritage. The potential for cultural tourism, in particular, presents an opportunity to attract international attention and appreciation for Sahrawi traditions, crafts, and lifestyles. This economic upliftment can empower local communities, enabling them to preserve and promote their cultural identity while contributing to the broader Moroccan economy.

Lastly, the global recognition of Sahrawi culture is supported by international diplomatic efforts advocating for Moroccan sovereignty. As Morocco continues to assert its claims over Western Sahara, the promotion of Sahrawi culture within this framework can serve as a powerful tool for enhancing regional stability and security. By fostering cultural exchange and collaboration, Morocco can ensure that Sahrawi voices are heard and valued, promoting a more inclusive governance model that respects local traditions and rights. This approach not only benefits the Sahrawi community but also enhances Morocco's image as a progressive nation committed to diversity and cultural heritage.

Chapter 12: The future prospects

The integration of Western Sahara with Morocco presents a compelling case that is supported by various key points. First and foremost, historical claims play a significant role in this discussion. The longstanding ties between Morocco and Western Sahara date back centuries, rooted in shared cultural, linguistic, and social values. These historical connections provide a foundation for the argument that Western Sahara is not merely a territory but an integral part of Morocco's national identity. This perspective is bolstered by the recognition of Morocco's historical governance over the region prior to colonial interventions, which disrupted traditional ties and territorial integrity.

From an economic standpoint, the benefits of integration with Morocco are substantial. The merging of resources and economic infrastructures can lead to increased investment opportunities and improved living standards for the Sahrawi people. Morocco has initiated numerous development projects aimed at enhancing infrastructure, creating jobs, and elevating the economic profile of the region. The potential for economic growth is further enhanced by Morocco's established trade networks and access to international markets, which can provide Western Sahara with a stronger economic foothold.

Cultural and linguistic ties between Sahrawis and Moroccans also reinforce the case for integration. The shared Arab-Berber heritage, language, and customs foster a sense of unity that transcends political boundaries. This cultural alignment can facilitate smoother governance and social cohesion, as both populations share similar values and traditions. By embracing these ties, Morocco can promote a more inclusive society that respects and celebrates the diverse identities within its borders.

In terms of security and stability, Moroccan governance is positioned to provide a framework for peace and order in the region. With a well-established security apparatus, Morocco can address potential threats and ensure the safety of all citizens, including those in Western Sahara. Moreover, the presence of Moroccan governance can help mitigate the risks associated with separatist movements and external influences that may destabilize the region. The emphasis on security aligns with broader regional interests, creating a safer environment for investment and development.

Finally, the international diplomatic support for Moroccan sovereignty over Western Sahara cannot be overlooked. Numerous countries and international organizations recognize Morocco's claims, which strengthens its position on the global stage. This support is crucial for fostering stability and encouraging development initiatives. Additionally, the potential for tourism and international recognition of Moroccan culture in Western Sahara can be significantly enhanced under Moroccan governance, promoting cultural exchange and economic benefits that arise from increased visitor interest. Through these combined factors, the case for Western Sahara's integration with Morocco is robust and multifaceted, highlighting the advantages of unity in diversity.

Vision for a unified future

The vision for a unified future in the context of Western Sahara's integration with Morocco is rooted in a shared identity, historical ties, and mutual benefits that can foster peace and prosperity for all. The historical claims of Morocco over Western Sahara are not merely political assertions; they are deeply embedded in the region's cultural and historical narratives. The long-standing connection between the Moroccan kingdom and the Sahrawi people is evident through centuries of shared governance, tribal affiliations, and economic interactions. Recognizing these historical ties is crucial in understanding the legitimacy of Moroccan sovereignty and the potential for a cohesive future.

Economically, integration with Morocco promises significant benefits for Western Sahara. The region is rich in natural resources, and aligning with Morocco can facilitate better management and utilization of these assets. Morocco's established infrastructure and economic frameworks can provide a solid foundation for development projects that will benefit the Sahrawi population. Investment in local industries, agriculture, and tourism can create job opportunities and enhance the overall standard of living. Moreover, as part of Morocco, Western Sahara can access broader markets, increasing its economic viability and sustainability.

Cultural and linguistic ties between the Sahrawis and Moroccans also play a pivotal role in this vision for unity. Both groups share a common heritage, with many Sahrawis identifying as part of the larger Moroccan cultural fabric. This shared identity can serve as a unifying force, promoting social cohesion and mutual understanding. By fostering cultural exchanges and educational initiatives, both communities can work towards a future where diversity is celebrated within a unified Moroccan identity. Such integration can lead to a richer cultural landscape, promoting tourism and international recognition of the unique Moroccan culture that includes Western Sahara.

Security and stability are paramount in a region marked by historical tensions. Under Moroccan governance, Western Sahara can benefit from enhanced security measures that a stable government can provide. Morocco's efforts to combat terrorism and promote regional stability can create a safer environment for the Sahrawi people. Furthermore, the Moroccan approach to governance emphasises local participation, which can empower Sahrawis to play an active role in their community's safety and development, thus fostering a sense of ownership and responsibility.

Finally, the integration of Western Sahara with Morocco aligns with international diplomatic support for Moroccan sovereignty. Many countries recognise Morocco's territorial integrity and the importance of stability in the region. This diplomatic backing can facilitate development initiatives and investment in infrastructure, enhancing the quality of life in Western Sahara. Shared religious and social values further underpin this integration, as both communities adhere to similar beliefs and customs. This common ground paves the way for collaborative approaches to human rights, environmental management, and resource sharing, ensuring that the future of Western Sahara is not only unified but also equitable and sustainable for all its inhabitants.

Chapter 13: How did all these problems start?

During the late 19th and early 20th centuries, European powers engaged in a frenzied race to carve up the African continent for their own economic and political gain. This period, known as the Scramble for Africa, saw a variety of tactics employed by European colonisers to control African territories. One common tactic was the use of military force to conquer and subjugate indigenous African populations. European powers often employed superior military technology and tactics to overpower African resistance movements and establish colonial administrations.

In addition to military force, European powers also utilised economic exploitation as a means of controlling African territories. European colonisers sought to extract valuable natural resources such as minerals, timber, and agricultural products from African lands for export to Europe. This economic exploitation often led to the impoverishment of African communities and the destruction of local economies. European powers also imposed unfair trade agreements and taxes on African populations, further exacerbating their economic exploitation.

Cultural erasure and assimilation under European rule

Cultural erasure and assimilation under European rule in Africa were a devastating consequence of the Scramble for Africa by European powers in the late 19th and early 20th centuries. European colonizers sought to impose their own cultural values and beliefs on African societies, erasing indigenous cultures and traditions in the process. This process of cultural assimilation was often carried out through the establishment of European schools, churches, and other institutions that sought to instill European ideals in the African population.

One of the primary methods of cultural erasure and assimilation was the role of European missionaries in the Scramble for Africa. Missionaries played a key role in spreading Christianity and Western values throughout Africa, often at the expense of indigenous belief systems. By converting Africans to Christianity and teaching them European languages and customs, missionaries played a significant role in erasing traditional African cultures and identities.

In addition to the cultural impact of European missionaries, the economic exploitation of African resources by European powers also played a significant role in the erasure of African cultures. European colonizers sought to exploit Africa's natural resources, often at great cost to the local population. This economic exploitation led to the destruction of traditional African livelihoods and economic systems, further eroding indigenous cultures and identities.

Despite the efforts of European powers to erase and assimilate African cultures, resistance movements against European colonisation emerged throughout Africa. These movements sought to preserve and protect indigenous cultures and traditions in the face of European imperialism. While many of these resistance movements were ultimately unsuccessful, they played a crucial role in preserving aspects of African culture in the face of European domination.

Chapter 14: The power of choice

The voices of the Saharawi and Moroccan people are crucial in shaping the future of Western Sahara and ensuring that their aspirations are recognised and respected. Both communities have unique cultural identities and histories that inform their perspectives on autonomy and self-determination. It is essential for Saharawi and Moroccan voices to lead discussions about their futures, as external influences often overlook the complexities of local realities. Empowering these voices means acknowledging their right to make decisions that affect their lives and communities without the imposition of foreign agendas.

Cultural identity plays a significant role in the narratives of both Saharawi and Moroccan populations. For the Saharawi, their connection to the land, nomadic heritage, and aspirations for independence are central to their identity. In contrast, Moroccans embrace a diverse cultural landscape that includes various ethnicities, languages, and traditions. Recognizing and respecting this cultural diversity is vital for fostering dialogue and understanding between the two communities. By prioritizing local voices, both groups can work towards a shared future that honours their distinct identities while promoting unity and cooperation.

Foreign intervention has often destabilised the region, complicating the quest for peace and autonomy. External powers may have interests that do not align with the needs and desires of the Saharawi and Moroccan people. Such interventions can exacerbate tensions and hinder progress toward dialogue and reconciliation. It is crucial for both communities to articulate their positions and advocate for solutions that prioritize their interests, rather than allowing outside forces to dictate the terms of engagement. By taking ownership of their narratives, Saharawi and Moroccan voices can challenge external influences and assert their right to self-determination.

The role of dialogue cannot be overstated, particularly among the youth of both communities. Young people are the future leaders and change-makers who will navigate the complexities of their shared history. Encouraging open communication between Saharawi and Moroccan youth can foster mutual respect, understanding, and collaboration. Initiatives that promote joint projects, cultural exchanges, and shared experiences can help to bridge divides and build trust. Empowering the younger generation to engage in constructive dialogue will lead to innovative solutions that honour the aspirations of both communities.

Ultimately, the path forward for Saharawi and Moroccan communities rests in their own hands. By amplifying local voices and fostering inclusive dialogue, both groups can work towards a future that reflects their shared values and aspirations. It is imperative that they take the lead in shaping their destinies, ensuring that their choices are driven by their own needs and dreams rather than the interests of outsiders. In doing so, they can pave the way for a more stable and harmonious region, rooted in respect for cultural identities and the principles of autonomy and self-determination.

Historical context of self-determination

The historical context of self-determination for the Saharawi people and their Moroccan counterparts is rooted in a complex interplay of colonial legacies, regional dynamics, and the quest for identity. The struggle for self-determination in Western Sahara emerged from the broader decolonization efforts that swept across Africa in the mid-20th century. As European powers withdrew from their colonies, the rights of indigenous populations to define their political futures gained prominence. For the Saharawi people, who have inhabited the region for centuries, this meant asserting their identity against the backdrop of Moroccan claims to sovereignty over the territory. This historical struggle underscores the importance of recognizing the Saharawi people's inherent right to choose their path without external imposition.

The notion of self-determination is not merely a political principle but also a vital aspect of cultural identity. For both Saharawi and Moroccan communities, the quest for autonomy is intertwined with their histories, languages, and traditions. The Saharawi people have developed a distinct cultural identity that reflects their nomadic heritage and resilience in the face of adversity. Conversely, Moroccan identity is shaped by a rich tapestry of Berber, Arab, and other influences, resulting in a diverse cultural landscape. The pursuit of self-determination allows both groups to embrace their unique identities while fostering a sense of belonging and community. This cultural dimension is essential for sustaining the narrative of self-determination, as it strengthens the resolve of both peoples to advocate for their rights and aspirations.

Foreign intervention has had significant ramifications for the stability of the region and the self-determination efforts of the Saharawi people. Various external actors, including former colonial powers and global superpowers, have historically influenced the trajectory of the Western Sahara conflict. Such interventions often reflect geopolitical interests rather than the needs and desires of the local populations. Consequently, the Saharawi struggle has at times been overshadowed by international diplomacy, sidelining the voices of those most affected. This situation highlights the necessity for Saharawi and Moroccan individuals to reclaim their agency, ensuring that their choices and perspectives guide the future of their communities rather than those imposed by outside forces.

In recognizing the importance of dialogue, particularly among the youth of Saharawi and Moroccan communities, the potential for peaceful coexistence and mutual understanding becomes evident. Young people are often at the forefront of social change and possess the energy and creativity to envision a future that transcends historical grievances. Encouraging dialogue between these two groups can foster a shared sense of purpose and identity, breaking down barriers built by years of conflict. Through collaborative efforts, youth can work towards addressing common challenges, promoting cultural exchange, and advocating for their rights in a way that is both constructive and inclusive.

Ultimately, the historical context of self-determination serves as a powerful reminder that the choice of the Saharawi and Moroccan people must remain at the forefront of any resolution to the conflict. Empowering these communities to make their own decisions about their futures is crucial for achieving lasting peace and stability in the region. By prioritizing local voices and encouraging unity among Saharawi and Moroccan youth, the path towards self-determination becomes not just a political aspiration but a communal journey towards embracing identity, culture, and shared values.

The importance of local agency

The importance of local agency in the context of the Saharawi and Moroccan communities cannot be overstated. Local agency refers to the capacity of individuals and groups within a community to make their own choices and decisions, particularly in relation to their cultural, social, and political identities. For the Saharawi people, who have long sought recognition and autonomy, the ability to assert their agency is crucial for ensuring their voices are heard and respected. Similarly, Moroccan citizens also play a vital role in shaping the narrative surrounding their own national identity and the future of their relationship with the Saharawi people. It is essential for both communities to engage in self-determination, as external influences can undermine their unique cultural identities and the potential for harmonious coexistence.

Cultural identity plays a key role in the autonomy of the Saharawi and Moroccan communities. Each group has its own rich history, traditions, and values that contribute to their unique identities. The Saharawi people, with their nomadic heritage and distinct language, have developed a strong sense of identity that is deeply intertwined with their struggle for self-determination. Meanwhile, Moroccans have their own diverse cultural landscape shaped by various influences, including Berber, Arab, and African traditions. Recognizing and respecting these cultural identities is essential for fostering mutual understanding and cooperation. When local communities take the lead in defining their cultural narratives, they can build more authentic connections with one another, leading to a more cohesive society.

Foreign intervention often complicates the dynamics between the Saharawi and Moroccan communities. External actors may impose their agendas, which can create divisions and exacerbate existing tensions. Historically, foreign powers have intervened in the region, often prioritizing their strategic interests over the voices of the local populations. This can lead to a lack of trust and further marginalization of the Saharawi people. By prioritizing local agency, both Saharawi and Moroccan communities can work towards solutions that are rooted in their own experiences and aspirations, rather than relying on outsiders who may not fully understand the complexities of the situation. Empowering local voices can contribute to long-term stability and peace in the region.

Dialogue between Saharawi and Moroccan youth is an essential aspect of fostering local agency and promoting understanding. Young people are often at the forefront of social change, and by engaging them in discussions about their shared futures, both communities can begin to bridge the gaps that have historically divided them. Initiatives that encourage dialogue can help youth from both sides to explore mutual interests, challenge stereotypes, and cultivate empathy. When young individuals come together to share their stories and aspirations, they create a platform for collaborative problem-solving that respects the autonomy of both communities. This grassroots approach can lead to innovative solutions and a shared commitment to peace and coexistence.

Ultimately, the importance of local agency for the Saharawi and Moroccan communities lies in their capacity to shape their own destinies. By prioritizing their voices and experiences, both groups can foster a sense of ownership over their cultural identities and futures. The path towards autonomy and mutual respect requires a commitment to dialogue, understanding, and collaboration. As these communities work together to assert their agency, they not only empower themselves but also contribute to a more stable and harmonious regional landscape. In choosing their own path, the Saharawi and Moroccan people can pave the way for a future that honours their unique identities while embracing the potential for coexistence.

Chapter 15: Cultural identity and autonomy

Understanding Saharawi cultural heritage is essential to grasp the complexities of identity and autonomy within the Saharawi and Moroccan communities. The Saharawi people, primarily residing in Western Sahara, possess a rich cultural heritage that is deeply tied to their nomadic traditions, oral histories, and unique customs. Their identity is shaped by centuries of adaptation to the harsh desert environment, creating a resilient community that values its traditions while also engaging with modern influences. Recognizing this heritage is crucial for both the Saharawi and Moroccan people, as it fosters a deeper understanding of their respective identities and aspirations.

The preservation and promotion of Saharawi cultural heritage serve as a foundation for the community's quest for autonomy. This heritage includes traditional music, dance, clothing, and crafts that reflect the Saharawi way of life. Engaging with these cultural elements enables the Saharawi people to assert their identity and articulate their vision for the future. As they seek to define their place in the world, it is vital that they remain the primary authors of their narrative, resisting external imposition that could dilute their cultural expressions. This emphasis on self-determination underscores the importance of Saharawi voices in discussions about their future.

The role of Moroccan culture in this dialogue cannot be overlooked. Morocco's rich history and diverse cultural tapestry contribute to a complex relationship with the Saharawi people. While both communities share geographic proximity and historical ties, their cultural differences highlight the necessity for mutual respect and understanding. It is crucial for Moroccan society to recognize the distinct cultural identity of the Saharawi, as this recognition can pave the way for constructive dialogue. By appreciating each other's cultural heritage, both communities can work towards a future that honours their unique identities while fostering cooperation and coexistence.

Foreign intervention has significantly impacted the cultural landscape of both Saharawi and Moroccan communities. External actors often impose narratives that can overshadow local voices, leading to misunderstandings and tensions. The influence of foreign powers can shift the focus away from grassroots movements and the authentic expressions of Saharawi culture. It is imperative that both Saharawi and Moroccan people reclaim their agency, ensuring that decisions regarding their future are made by those who live within the region. By prioritising local perspectives, they can create a more stable and harmonious environment that respects their cultural heritages.

For the youth of both communities, understanding and appreciating each other's cultural heritage is vital for fostering dialogue and collaboration. Engaging with Saharawi traditions can inspire Moroccan youth to advocate for a more inclusive narrative that respects diverse identities. Likewise, Saharawi youth can benefit from understanding Moroccan culture, facilitating mutual respect and shared goals. By promoting cultural exchange and dialogue, both groups can empower each other, working together to choose a path that honours their histories while building a future based on collaboration and understanding.

Moroccan identity in a globalised world

Moroccan identity is a multifaceted construct that has evolved through centuries of cultural exchange, historical events, and socio-political dynamics. In the context of globalization, this identity faces both challenges and opportunities. The influence of foreign cultures through media, technology, and commerce has led to a blending of traditions and practices, which can dilute the essence of what it means to be Moroccan. However, this global interconnectedness also offers a platform for the Moroccan and Saharawi people to assert their unique identities and narratives in the face of external pressures. As they navigate this complex landscape, it is crucial for Moroccans and Saharawis to define their identities on their own terms, free from the imposition of external forces.

The question of autonomy is central to the discourse on Moroccan and Saharawi identities. For both communities, the path to self-determination is essential not only for cultural preservation but also for political agency. The Saharawi people, in particular, have long sought recognition and autonomy, and their voices must be at the forefront of discussions regarding their future. It is imperative that decisions affecting these communities are made by the people themselves rather than dictated by foreign powers or external organizations. This autonomy is not just about political rights; it encompasses the preservation of cultural heritage, language, and traditions that are integral to their identities.

Foreign intervention in the region has historically impacted the stability of both Morocco and Western Sahara. External influences can exacerbate tensions, undermine local governance, and hinder genuine dialogue between the Moroccan and Saharawi communities. The consequences of such interventions often lead to a misrepresentation of local aspirations and grievances on the global stage. It is essential for both Moroccans and Saharawis to engage in constructive discussions that clarify their perspectives without the distortion of outside interests. This self-representation is vital for fostering regional stability and ensuring that the needs and desires of the people are prioritized.

Dialogue between Moroccan and Saharawi youth holds particular significance in shaping a shared future. These young individuals represent the next generation of leaders and thinkers, and their interactions can pave the way for reconciliation and mutual understanding. By engaging in open conversations about identity, culture, and aspirations, they can challenge stereotypes and build bridges that transcend historical divides. Promoting platforms for dialogue fosters empathy and collaboration, allowing both communities to find common ground while respecting their distinct identities.

Ultimately, the journey towards a more cohesive Moroccan identity within a globalized world lies in the hands of its people. The narratives of both Moroccans and Saharawis must be actively shaped by their own experiences and aspirations, free from the influence of external entities. Empowering these communities to make their own choices is crucial for ensuring that their cultural identities flourish amidst globalization. By valuing local voices and encouraging dialogue, both communities can navigate the complexities of modernity while preserving the rich tapestry of their heritage.

The intersection of culture and autonomy

The concept of autonomy is deeply intertwined with cultural identity, particularly for the Saharawi and Moroccan communities. Both groups have rich cultural heritages that shape their identities and inform their aspirations for self-determination. The Saharawi people, with their distinct traditions, languages, and societal structures, seek the opportunity to express their cultural identity freely. Similarly, Moroccans possess their own diverse cultural backgrounds, influenced by Berber, Arab, and other traditions. Understanding this intersection of culture and autonomy is crucial, as it underscores the importance of allowing these communities to make their own choices regarding their futures.

Cultural identity acts as a powerful catalyst for autonomy. For the Saharawi, their cultural practices and historical narratives are central to their claims for recognition and self-governance. The preservation of their language, art, and customs is not merely a matter of heritage; it is intertwined with their political aspirations. On the Moroccan side, the recognition and respect for cultural diversity enhance the national narrative, allowing different groups to coexist while contributing to a unified identity. When both communities are empowered to define their cultural identities, they are better positioned to assert their autonomy and work towards coexistence.

Foreign intervention often complicates the pursuit of autonomy and cultural identity. External actors may impose solutions that overlook the nuanced realities of the Saharawi and Moroccan contexts. Such interventions can exacerbate tensions, undermine local agency, and disregard the voices of those most affected by the conflict. It is critical that any resolution acknowledges the importance of local perspectives and the need for an inclusive dialogue that prioritizes the desires of both the Saharawi and Moroccan people. By sidelining outside influences, these communities can focus on fostering a peaceful resolution grounded in mutual respect and understanding.

The importance of dialogue between Saharawi and Moroccan youth cannot be overstated. Young people are the future leaders who will shape the trajectory of their communities. By engaging in open conversations, they can bridge divides, share experiences, and cultivate a shared vision for a peaceful coexistence. Initiatives aimed at fostering dialogue can empower youth to advocate for their rights and cultural identity while also recognizing the cultural richness of the other. This collaborative approach can help mitigate the impacts of foreign intervention and build a foundation for sustainable autonomy that respects both Saharawi and Moroccan identities.

Ultimately, the intersection of culture and autonomy is a pivotal area of focus for the Saharawi and Moroccan communities. By embracing their cultural identities and asserting their rights to self-determination, these groups can chart a path toward a more stable and harmonious future. It is essential that the decisions regarding their futures remain in the hands of the Saharawi and Moroccan people, free from the influence of external powers. This empowerment not only strengthens their cultural identities but also paves the way for a more peaceful coexistence, fostering a regional dynamic that respects diversity and promotes understanding.

Chapter 16: Foreign intervention and its consequences

The historical context of foreign involvement in the Saharawi and Moroccan regions reveals a complex tapestry of interactions that have shaped the identities and political landscapes of the people. Beginning with the colonial era, the Spanish and French colonial powers exerted significant influence over the territories that now encompass Western Sahara and Morocco. The imposition of foreign rule disrupted traditional governance structures and introduced new political dynamics, which continue to resonate in contemporary discussions about autonomy and self-determination. This historical backdrop underscores the importance of recognising that the Saharawi and Moroccan peoples possess the agency to determine their own futures, free from external pressures.

In the wake of decolonisation, the struggle for independence in the Saharawi territories became a focal point for foreign involvement. Various nations and international organizations began to take interest in the conflict, often aligning with one side or the other based on strategic interests, economic advantages, or ideological sympathies. This influx of foreign influence complicated the pursuit of a peaceful resolution, as external actors sometimes prioritized their geopolitical agendas over the voices and needs of the Saharawi and Moroccan populations. The ongoing situation illustrates how foreign intervention can undermine the prospects for dialogue and reconciliation between the two communities.

The impact of foreign involvement extends beyond immediate political ramifications to include cultural dimensions as well. International actors have often imposed narratives that shape perceptions of the conflict, influencing public opinion both regionally and globally. These narratives frequently overshadow the rich cultural identities of the Saharawi and Moroccan peoples, reducing their experiences to mere pawns in a larger geopolitical game. The need for Saharawi and Moroccan voices to be at the forefront of discussions about their identities and futures is paramount, as it is through their own narratives that a more nuanced understanding of the situation can emerge.

Moreover, the historical overview reveals the dual-edged nature of foreign intervention in relation to regional stability. While some foreign powers have sought to mediate and provide support for peace initiatives, others have exacerbated tensions by taking sides or failing to recognize the legitimate aspirations of both communities. This has often led to a cycle of mistrust and conflict that hinders the development of sustainable solutions. For true stability to be achieved, it is essential for the Saharawi and Moroccan peoples to engage in dialogue, fostering understanding and collaboration that is rooted in their shared histories and aspirations.

Ultimately, the path forward for both Saharawi and Moroccan communities lies within their ability to reclaim their narratives and make decisions that reflect their unique identities and aspirations. As the historical overview illustrates, foreign involvement has often complicated matters, but it is the voices of the Saharawi and Moroccan youth that hold the key to a collaborative future. By prioritizing dialogue and mutual respect, both communities can work toward a more harmonious coexistence, one that honours their cultural identities while also acknowledging the importance of autonomy in shaping their destinies.

Case Studies of intervention in the region

Case studies of intervention in the Saharawi and Moroccan regions illustrate the complex interplay of local agency, cultural identity, and the need for autonomous decision-making. Historical interventions by foreign powers have often disrupted local dynamics, imposing external narratives that do not necessarily resonate with the realities of the Saharawi and Moroccan peoples. For instance, the influence of colonial powers in the early 20th century laid the groundwork for ongoing tensions. This historical backdrop highlights the importance of allowing the Saharawi and Moroccan communities to define their own futures without the overshadowing influence of outsiders.

One significant example is the role of international organizations in mediating the conflict. The United Nations has attempted to facilitate dialogue between the Saharawi and Moroccan governments, often emphasizing the need for a referendum on self-determination. While well-intentioned, such interventions can sometimes overlook the unique cultural identities and aspirations of the people involved. This approach raises questions about the effectiveness of external mediation in resolving disputes that are deeply rooted in local contexts. It underscores the necessity for Saharawi and Moroccan voices to lead discussions about their futures, ensuring that any solutions are culturally relevant and widely accepted.

Another case study reveals the impact of economic interventions on regional stability. Various foreign investments in Moroccan infrastructure have been met with skepticism from Saharawi activists who argue that these developments often benefit external stakeholders rather than the local population. The resulting economic disparities can exacerbate tensions and foster resentment among the Saharawi people. This situation highlights the critical need for inclusive economic strategies that prioritize local needs and integrate the perspectives of both Saharawi and Moroccan communities. Such approaches not only promote fairness but also enhance the prospects for lasting peace and stability in the region.

Youth engagement has emerged as a vital element in fostering dialogue between Saharawi and Moroccan communities. Initiatives that empower young people to share their experiences and aspirations have proven effective in bridging divides. Programs that facilitate cultural exchanges and collaborative projects can create a sense of shared identity and mutual respect. These interactions are crucial for building a future where both Saharawi and Moroccan youth can advocate for their rights and interests collectively, rather than being influenced by external narratives that may not reflect their realities. The empowerment of youth is essential to shaping a narrative that emphasizes autonomy and self-determination.

In conclusion, the case studies of intervention in the region underscore the importance of local agency in addressing the complexities of the Saharawi and Moroccan relationship. The historical context of foreign interference serves as a reminder of the necessity for the Saharawi and Moroccan peoples to reclaim their narratives and make their own choices. By fostering dialogue and cooperation, particularly among youth, the communities can work towards a future defined by cultural identity and autonomy. This approach not only honours the rich heritage of both groups but also paves the way for a more stable and harmonious regional landscape.

The Impact on local governance and stability

The governance structures in both Saharawi and Moroccan territories have been significantly shaped by local dynamics, yet they are often influenced by external actors. The ongoing conflict over Western Sahara has led to a complex interplay between local governance and foreign interests. For the Saharawi people, local governance is rooted in their aspirations for autonomy and self-determination, which are essential to their cultural identity. In contrast, Moroccan governance structures reflect a centralized approach that has often sidelined the voices of the Saharawi population. This disconnect poses challenges to stability, as it creates an environment where grievances may fester and escalate into conflict.

Local governance in the Saharawi regions, primarily represented by the Sahrawi Arab Democratic Republic (SADR), emphasizes communal decision-making and participation. This model fosters a sense of ownership among the Saharawi people, allowing them to navigate their sociopolitical landscape in a manner that aligns with their cultural values. However, the effectiveness of this governance is frequently undermined by external pressures and the lack of international recognition. The legitimacy of the SADR is challenged by Morocco's claims over the territory, creating a governance vacuum that complicates the pursuit of peace and stability.

Conversely, Moroccan governance is characterized by a top-down approach that often marginalizes local voices, particularly in the Saharawi regions. This imbalance can breed resentment and a sense of exclusion among Saharawis, leading to tensions that threaten regional stability. The Moroccan government's efforts to integrate the Saharawi population into its national identity have been met with skepticism, as many Saharawis view these initiatives as superficial attempts to dilute their cultural identity. This fracture in local governance structures contributes to ongoing instability, as it fails to address the core issues of autonomy and self-determination.

Foreign intervention in the Western Sahara conflict has further complicated local governance and stability. External actors often prioritize geopolitical interests over the voices of the Saharawi and Moroccan people, leading to policies that do not reflect the realities on the ground. This interference can exacerbate tensions and hinder the peace process, as local populations feel their agency is undermined. The emphasis on external mediation can detract from the importance of homegrown solutions that emerge from dialogue among Saharawi and Moroccan communities, which are crucial for fostering long-term stability.

Encouraging dialogue between Saharawi and Moroccan youth is essential for rebuilding trust and cooperation in the region. Young people, who are often more open to new ideas and perspectives, can serve as catalysts for change by fostering a shared understanding of each community's aspirations. By creating spaces for dialogue, both communities can work towards a future that respects cultural identities and promotes autonomy. Empowering local voices to shape their governance structures will ultimately lead to a more stable and peaceful coexistence, demonstrating that the path forward must be determined by the people who inhabit the land, rather than imposed by external forces.

Chapter 17: The role of youth in shaping the future

Engaging Saharawi youth in dialogue is a crucial step towards fostering understanding and cooperation between Saharawi and Moroccan communities. The active participation of young people in conversations about their future is vital, as they represent the next generation of leaders and decision-makers. By providing a platform for these dialogues, both communities can address their shared challenges, promote cultural identity, and work towards achieving greater autonomy. It is essential that these discussions are led by Saharawi and Moroccan youth themselves, emphasizing their agency and capacity to shape their own destinies without external interference.

Cultural identity plays a significant role in the lives of both Saharawi and Moroccan youth. Engaging in dialogue allows young people to express their unique cultural backgrounds while also recognizing the commonalities that exist between them. Through collaborative storytelling and cultural exchanges, they can celebrate their heritage and explore their identities together. This mutual understanding can help dismantle stereotypes and prejudices, paving the way for a more cohesive society where both groups can coexist harmoniously. The dialogue can also reinforce the importance of cultural preservation, ensuring that the voices and traditions of the Saharawi people are respected and valued.

The impact of foreign intervention in the region has often complicated the relationship between Saharawi and Moroccan communities. External influences can exacerbate tensions and create divisions, diverting attention away from the essential conversations that need to take place. Engaging Saharawi youth in dialogue helps to counteract these influences by fostering a sense of ownership over their narratives and future. By prioritising local voices, these young people can advocate for solutions that reflect their needs and aspirations rather than those imposed by outsiders. Encouraging self-determination is key to building a stable and peaceful future for both communities.

In addition to addressing cultural identity and foreign intervention, dialogue between Saharawi and Moroccan youth can serve as a powerful tool for regional stability. Collaborative initiatives that promote peace and understanding can help mitigate conflicts and foster a sense of unity. When young people from both sides come together to discuss their hopes, dreams, and concerns, they establish personal connections that transcend political boundaries. These relationships can lead to grassroots movements aimed at promoting peace and cooperation, ultimately contributing to a more stable and prosperous region.

To ensure the success of these dialogues, it is essential to create inclusive and safe spaces where all voices are heard and respected. Facilitators should be trained to guide discussions in a way that encourages participation from everyone, especially marginalized groups within both communities. By nurturing an environment of trust and openness, Saharawi and Moroccan youth can engage in meaningful conversations that empower them to take ownership of their futures. This empowerment is crucial, as it reinforces the notion that it is up to the Saharawi and Moroccan people to make their own choices, shaping a path that reflects their shared values and aspirations.

Moroccan youth perspectives on the conflict

Moroccan youth hold a unique position in understanding the complexities of the Western Sahara conflict, shaped by their cultural identities and the socio-political landscape of their nation. As the next generation grows up amid ongoing tensions, their perspectives are pivotal in framing the narrative of autonomy and self-determination. Many young Moroccans express a desire for dialogue and collaboration with their Saharawi counterparts, emphasizing that the resolution of the conflict should arise from within the region rather than being dictated by external powers. This sentiment echoes a broader understanding that the voices of both Moroccan and Saharawi communities must be prioritized in the quest for lasting peace.

The cultural identity of Moroccan youth is deeply intertwined with the historical context of the Western Sahara. Many young Moroccans view their national identity as inclusive of Saharawi people, recognizing the shared heritage and cultural ties that bind the two communities. This perspective fosters a sense of solidarity, as youth strive to transcend the political divisions imposed by previous generations. They advocate for a narrative that celebrates the rich cultural tapestry of Morocco, which includes Saharawi traditions, languages, and histories. By embracing this shared identity, Moroccan youth aim to create a foundation for mutual understanding and respect, essential components in any dialogue aimed at resolving the conflict.

The impact of foreign intervention on regional stability is a significant concern among Moroccan youth. Many express skepticism about the motivations of external actors, believing that their involvement often exacerbates tensions rather than alleviating them. This perspective highlights a growing awareness that solutions must be locally driven, focusing on the needs and aspirations of the people directly affected by the conflict. Young Moroccans emphasize that foreign powers should not dictate terms or impose solutions, as this undermines the agency of both Moroccan and Saharawi communities. Instead, they call for a re-evaluation of foreign policies that prioritize dialogue and collaboration, fostering an environment where both groups can express their aspirations freely.

Dialogue between Saharawi and Moroccan youth is increasingly recognized as essential for building bridges and fostering understanding. Many young people from both sides have initiated grassroots movements aimed at facilitating conversations about their shared future. These initiatives often take the form of workshops, cultural exchanges, and collaborative projects that underscore common goals such as education and economic development. Participants find that engaging with one another humanizes the conflict, moving beyond political rhetoric to focus on personal stories and experiences. This grassroots dialogue empowers youth to take ownership of their narratives, reinforcing the belief that they are best positioned to shape their destinies.

In conclusion, the perspectives of Moroccan youth on the Western Sahara conflict reveal a collective yearning for peace, understanding, and autonomy. They recognize that the path forward must be charted by the people who inhabit the region, rather than by outsiders with their own agendas. By fostering dialogue and embracing a shared cultural identity, Moroccan and Saharawi youth can work together to redefine the narrative surrounding the conflict. As they confront challenges and envision a more cooperative future, it becomes increasingly clear that their voices are crucial in the ongoing pursuit of self-determination and regional stability.

Collaborative initiatives for peacebuilding

Collaborative initiatives for peacebuilding between the Saharawi and Moroccan communities are crucial in fostering understanding, promoting dialogue, and ultimately paving the way for a sustainable resolution to the ongoing conflict. Both communities possess rich cultural identities that shape their perspectives and aspirations. It is essential that these initiatives are led by the Saharawi and Moroccan people themselves, as they are best positioned to navigate their unique histories and cultural contexts. Empowering local voices not only enhances the legitimacy of peacebuilding efforts but also ensures that solutions are tailored to the specific needs and aspirations of both communities.

One notable example of a collaborative initiative is the establishment of joint cultural exchanges that celebrate the shared heritage of the Saharawi and Moroccan peoples. These exchanges can take the form of art exhibitions, music festivals, and culinary events that highlight the commonalities between the two cultures. By engaging in these cultural activities, participants have the opportunity to break down barriers, dispel stereotypes, and foster mutual respect. Such initiatives are vital in creating a sense of community and interconnectedness, which is essential for long-term peacebuilding.

Another important aspect of collaborative initiatives is the involvement of youth from both communities. Young people are often at the forefront of social change, and their engagement in peacebuilding efforts can have a profound impact. Programs that promote dialogue and cooperation among Saharawi and Moroccan youth can empower them to take ownership of their future. Workshops, forums, and joint projects that encourage collaboration and teamwork can help to bridge divides, nurturing a generation that values dialogue over conflict. By equipping youth with the tools for constructive communication, these initiatives can lay the groundwork for a more peaceful coexistence.

The role of technology in facilitating these collaborative initiatives cannot be overlooked. Social media platforms and online forums provide opportunities for Saharawi and Moroccan individuals to connect, share their stories, and engage in meaningful discussions. Virtual spaces can transcend geographical boundaries, allowing for greater interaction and understanding. Harnessing technology as a tool for dialogue can enable the younger generations to engage in peacebuilding efforts without the constraints of traditional barriers, fostering a sense of solidarity and shared purpose.

Ultimately, the path towards peacebuilding in the Saharawi and Moroccan contexts must be led by the voices of the people directly affected by the conflict. Outsider intervention often complicates the situation and can undermine local agency. By prioritizing collaborative initiatives that centre on cultural identity, youth engagement, and the utilization of technology, both communities can work towards a future defined by autonomy and mutual respect. Empowering Saharawi and Moroccan voices not only honours their distinct identities but also reinforces the belief that they are the architects of their own destiny.

Chapter 18: Building bridges through dialogue

The importance of inter-community communication between the Saharawi and Moroccan populations cannot be overstated. Both communities share a complex history marked by cultural ties, shared challenges, and a mutual desire for recognition and autonomy. Effective communication fosters understanding, dispels myths, and builds trust, which are essential for any meaningful dialogue aimed at resolving conflicts and finding common ground. In a region where external influences often dominate discussions, it becomes even more critical for the Saharawi and Moroccan voices to take centre stage in shaping their shared future.

Cultural identity plays a pivotal role in the lives of both the Saharawi and Moroccan people. Each community has its unique traditions, languages, and historical narratives that deserve acknowledgment and respect. By engaging in open dialogues, individuals from both groups can highlight their cultural heritage while also recognizing the value in each other's identities. This exchange not only enriches the social fabric of the region but also fosters a sense of belonging and pride among the youth, who are the future leaders and custodians of these cultures. When young people understand and appreciate each other's backgrounds, they are more likely to collaborate toward collective goals.

In contrast, foreign intervention often exacerbates existing tensions and hinders progress toward regional stability. Outsiders may impose solutions that do not reflect the realities or aspirations of the Saharawi and Moroccan peoples. This can lead to a cycle of dependency and resentment, undermining the agency of local communities. By prioritizing inter-community communication, both groups can reclaim their narrative and advocate for solutions that reflect their unique circumstances. This approach empowers the Saharawi and Moroccan people to make their own choices regarding governance, development, and social cohesion, rather than allowing external forces to dictate their paths.

Moreover, the importance of dialogue between the youth of both communities cannot be understated. Young people are often the most affected by political decisions and conflict, yet they also hold the potential to drive change. Facilitating platforms for Saharawi and Moroccan youth to engage in constructive conversations can lead to innovative solutions and a collaborative spirit. By fostering friendships and partnerships, they can work together to address shared challenges, such as education, employment, and social justice. This grassroots approach to dialogue can build long-lasting relationships that transcend political boundaries and promote a culture of peace.

Ultimately, the path toward empowerment for both the Saharawi and Moroccan people lies in their ability to communicate effectively with one another. By prioritizing inter-community dialogue, they can assert their rights to self-determination and cultural expression while also fostering a sense of unity and shared purpose. As they navigate the complexities of their relationship, it is crucial that they remain at the forefront of discussions regarding their futures. In doing so, they can create a more inclusive, resilient, and stable region where both communities thrive together.

Platforms for dialogue between cultures

Platforms for dialogue between cultures play a crucial role in fostering understanding and collaboration between the Saharawi and Moroccan communities. These platforms serve as spaces where individuals from both groups can come together to share their experiences, challenges, and aspirations. By facilitating open communication, these dialogues can help dismantle stereotypes and build mutual respect. The creation of such platforms should be driven by the people of Saharawi and Morocco themselves, ensuring that their voices are at the forefront of discussions that affect their lives.

In recent years, various initiatives have emerged that aim to bridge the gap between Saharawi and Moroccan youth. These include cultural exchange programs, joint artistic projects, and community-led forums that encourage dialogue on shared interests and common goals. By participating in these initiatives, young people can develop a deeper appreciation for each other's cultures while also recognizing the complexities of their historical and political contexts. Empowering youth to engage in these conversations is essential for nurturing a generation that values cooperation over conflict.

The importance of cultural identity in these dialogues cannot be overstated. For both Saharawi and Moroccan communities, cultural identity serves as a foundation for individual and collective empowerment. By engaging in dialogue, participants can explore how their cultural backgrounds shape their perspectives and identities. This exploration can lead to a more nuanced understanding of each group's unique narratives and challenges. As these identities are acknowledged and respected, the potential for collaboration and solidarity increases, paving the way for constructive engagement.

Foreign intervention has often complicated the relationship between Saharawi and Moroccan communities, leading to tensions and misunderstandings. External influences can exacerbate divisions and hinder the development of authentic dialogue. Therefore, it is imperative that the people of Saharawi and Morocco take ownership of their narratives and interactions. By prioritizing their own voices and experiences, they can create a more stable and harmonious environment that resists external manipulation and promotes genuine understanding.

Ultimately, the success of dialogue platforms lies in the commitment of both communities to engage in honest and respectful conversations. When Saharawi and Moroccan youth come together to discuss their hopes and concerns, they lay the groundwork for a future based on mutual understanding and cooperation. By fostering these dialogues, both groups can empower themselves to make informed choices about their paths forward, creating a more inclusive and peaceful coexistence.

Success stories of collaboration

Success stories of collaboration between Saharawi and Moroccan communities demonstrate the potential for unity and shared purpose despite historical tensions. These narratives highlight grassroots initiatives that have emerged from within the region, showcasing the power of local actors to forge paths toward mutual understanding and cooperation. By focusing on shared interests and goals, community members have found ways to engage in dialogue and collaboration that transcend political divides. These stories serve as a testament to the resilience and determination of both Saharawi and Moroccan people to reclaim their narratives and build a brighter future together.

One notable example is the emergence of joint cultural initiatives that celebrate the rich heritage of both communities. Art exhibitions, music festivals, and culinary fairs have brought together artists, musicians, and chefs from both sides, creating a space for cultural exchange and appreciation. These events not only foster a sense of community but also serve as platforms for dialogue, allowing participants to share their experiences and perspectives. By emphasizing common cultural threads, these initiatives help to dismantle stereotypes and promote a shared identity that transcends political affiliations.

In education, collaborative programs have emerged that focus on empowering youth from both communities. Workshops and exchange programs have been developed, encouraging young Saharawi and Moroccan students to work together on projects that address local challenges. These initiatives promote teamwork, innovation, and leadership skills, enabling the next generation to envision a future where collaboration is the norm rather than the exception. By investing in youth, both communities are taking proactive steps to shape their destinies, reinforcing the notion that lasting change must come from within.

Furthermore, the impact of joint environmental projects cannot be overlooked. Communities have come together to address pressing issues such as water scarcity, desertification, and sustainable agriculture. By pooling their knowledge and resources, Saharawi and Moroccan farmers have successfully implemented practices that benefit both communities while fostering a spirit of cooperation. These environmental initiatives not only enhance regional resilience but also reinforce the idea that collaborative efforts can lead to tangible improvements in quality of life, reflecting a shared commitment to the land and future generations.

Ultimately, the success stories of collaboration between Saharawi and Moroccan communities highlight the importance of dialogue, understanding, and shared action. As both groups navigate their complex histories and identities, these narratives serve as powerful reminders that they hold the keys to their futures. By choosing to collaborate rather than confront, they can cultivate an environment of respect and cooperation that transcends borders. Such efforts not only empower local voices but also challenge the notion that solutions must come from external forces, reinforcing the belief that the future of Saharawi and Moroccan communities lies in their own hands.

Chapter 19: Pathways to empowerment

Education and Empowerment Initiatives

Education and empowerment initiatives play a crucial role in shaping the future of Saharawi and Moroccan communities. These initiatives are designed to promote cultural identity and enhance autonomy, enabling individuals to make informed choices that reflect their unique backgrounds and aspirations. By focusing on education, both formal and informal, these programs foster a sense of self-worth and agency among Saharawi and Moroccan youth, empowering them to take charge of their narratives and destinies. This empowerment is essential, as it counters the influence of external forces that may seek to impose solutions that do not resonate with the realities of the local populace.

In the Saharawi context, education is not merely about academic knowledge but also about cultural preservation and identity. Initiatives that integrate Saharawi history, language, and traditions into the education system help young people connect with their heritage. This connection fosters pride in their identity, encouraging them to advocate for their rights and aspirations. Additionally, empowering Saharawi youth through education equips them with the skills needed to engage effectively in dialogue with Moroccan counterparts. Such interactions can bridge divides and foster mutual understanding, allowing for collaborative efforts toward common goals.

On the Moroccan side, educational programs focused on promoting inclusivity and understanding of the Saharawi perspective are equally important. By encouraging Moroccan youth to learn about Saharawi culture and the socio-political landscape, these initiatives create opportunities for empathy and solidarity. This understanding is vital in fostering a culture of dialogue, where young people can express their views and concerns without fear of marginalization. When empowered through education, Moroccan youth can become advocates for peace and cooperation, recognizing the shared interests that can pave the way toward a more stable and harmonious region.

Foreign intervention often complicates matters, as external actors may impose their interests rather than allowing local voices to guide the path forward. Education and empowerment initiatives serve as a counterbalance to this influence, reinforcing the notion that the Saharawi and Moroccan people are best positioned to determine their futures. By prioritizing local agency, these initiatives help build resilience against external pressures, ensuring that the solutions developed are grounded in the communities they affect. Ultimately, the path to stability in the region lies in the hands of its people, who must have the tools and opportunities to shape their own destinies.

The significance of dialogue between Saharawi and Moroccan youth cannot be overstated. Education and empowerment initiatives provide the foundation for such dialogue, fostering an environment where young people can come together to discuss their hopes, fears, and aspirations. Through workshops, cultural exchanges, and collaborative projects, these initiatives create spaces for meaningful interaction. As young people engage in constructive conversations, they can challenge stereotypes, build relationships, and work toward a collective vision of peace and cooperation. In this way, education becomes a powerful catalyst for change, enabling both Saharawi and Moroccan communities to navigate their shared future with confidence and mutual respect.

Grassroots movements and their impact

Grassroots movements play a crucial role in shaping the political and social landscapes of communities, particularly in regions like Western Sahara and Morocco. These movements often emerge from the collective aspirations of local populations who seek to assert their rights, cultural identity, and autonomy. In the context of the Saharawi and Moroccan peoples, grassroots activism has been instrumental in fostering a sense of agency and empowerment. By organizing locally, these communities can address issues that are often overlooked by external actors, ensuring that their voices are heard and their needs are prioritized.

The Saharawi people, in particular, have demonstrated resilience through their grassroots movements, seeking to raise awareness about their quest for self-determination and cultural preservation. Organizations such as the Saharawi Youth Union and various cultural associations have mobilized efforts to educate both local and international audiences about their plight. These movements emphasize the importance of Saharawi identity and heritage, advocating for recognition and respect from the Moroccan state and the international community. By highlighting their unique cultural practices, they reinforce the narrative that the Saharawi people are entitled to make their own choices about their future.

In contrast, Moroccan grassroots movements have emerged as a response to various socio-economic challenges, including unemployment, corruption, and the demand for greater political freedoms. These movements often unite diverse groups within Morocco, fostering dialogue and collaboration among citizens who share common goals. The interplay between Saharawi and Moroccan grassroots efforts is vital, as it can lead to a more inclusive approach to regional stability and peace. Both communities must engage in constructive dialogue to address their grievances and explore potential pathways toward coexistence.

Foreign intervention has historically complicated the dynamics between the Saharawi and Moroccan peoples, often undermining local efforts to find resolution. External actors, whether they are states or international organizations, can impose solutions that do not reflect the realities or desires of the affected communities. This has led to a growing sentiment among Saharawi and Moroccan activists that it is essential for their peoples to take charge of their destinies. By focusing on grassroots solutions, they can create sustainable change that aligns with their cultural identities and aspirations, rather than relying on external forces that may not fully understand the complexities of the region.

Ultimately, the importance of dialogue among Saharawi and Moroccan youth cannot be overstated. These young individuals are the future of their communities and have the potential to bridge divides through collaboration and mutual understanding. Grassroots movements that encourage youth participation can foster a climate of empathy and shared purpose. By engaging with each other, they can work towards solutions that honour both Saharawi and Moroccan identities, paving the way for a more stable and harmonious future in the region. The empowerment of local voices is essential in crafting a path that reflects the true aspirations of the Saharawi and Moroccan peoples.

The future of autonomy and identity

The future of autonomy and identity for Saharawi and Moroccan people hinges on the ability of these communities to assert their rights and choose their own paths without external interference. The Saharawi people, with their unique cultural heritage and historical claims to their land, must navigate their aspirations for self-determination in the face of longstanding political complexities. Similarly, Moroccans, who share a rich tapestry of cultural identities, must recognize the intrinsic value of allowing their Saharawi counterparts to express their desires and needs. This process of self-identification and autonomy is essential not only for the individuals involved but also for fostering a stable and harmonious future in the region.

Cultural identity plays a pivotal role in shaping the future of both Saharawi and Moroccan communities. The Saharawi people possess a distinct cultural heritage that includes language, music, and traditions that are integral to their identity. This cultural richness must be preserved and promoted, serving as a foundation for their quest for autonomy. In Morocco, the acknowledgment of diverse cultural identities can strengthen national unity while allowing various groups to thrive. By embracing cultural plurality, both communities can create an environment where dialogue and mutual respect flourish, ultimately leading to a more cohesive society.

Foreign intervention has historically disrupted the stability of the Saharawi and Moroccan regions, often complicating the prospects for peace and autonomy. External actors, driven by political or economic interests, can exacerbate tensions by failing to respect the voices and rights of local populations. The future of these communities will likely be shaped by their ability to resist manipulation by outside forces. Engaging in self-determined dialogue and establishing strong grassroots movements can empower Saharawi and Moroccan voices to reclaim their narratives and influence the political landscape that affects their lives.

Dialogue between Saharawi and Moroccan youth is crucial for building bridges that foster understanding and cooperation. Young people, as the leaders of tomorrow, hold the potential to dismantle stereotypes and preconceived notions that have historically divided the two communities. Initiatives that promote joint cultural exchanges, educational collaborations, and shared community projects can encourage youth to find common ground. By fostering relationships built on trust and shared experiences, the future generations can pave the way for a more inclusive society where both Saharawi and Moroccan identities are respected and valued.

Ultimately, the future of autonomy and identity for Saharawi and Moroccan people lies in their hands. As they navigate the challenges posed by historical grievances and external influences, the importance of self-determination will become increasingly evident. By prioritizing local voices, embracing cultural diversity, and engaging in constructive dialogue, both communities can work towards a future that honours their unique histories and aspirations. The journey ahead may be complex, but it is one that the Saharawi and Moroccan peoples must undertake together, forging a path that reflects their collective identity and choices.

Chapter 20: Conclusion: A shared vision for the future

In "Choosing Our Path: Empowering Saharawi and Moroccan Voices," various key themes emerge that underscore the importance of self-determination for both the Saharawi and Moroccan peoples. Central to this discourse is the assertion that it is the responsibility of these communities to make their own choices, rather than allowing external forces to dictate their futures. This emphasis on local agency highlights the need for the Saharawi and Moroccan populations to take charge of their narratives, ensuring that their unique cultural identities and aspirations shape the political landscape of the region.

Cultural identity plays a pivotal role in this discussion, as both Saharawi and Moroccan communities possess rich traditions and histories that inform their worldviews. The interplay of these identities has been influenced by historical events, colonial legacies, and contemporary socio-political dynamics. Recognising and celebrating this diversity is essential for building a cohesive society that respects the rights and identities of all its members. Through fostering a sense of pride in their cultural heritage, both groups can work collaboratively towards a future that honours their distinct identities while also seeking common ground.

External influences have historically disrupted the social and political fabric of the region, often exacerbating tensions between the Saharawi and Moroccan communities. By examining the consequences of such interventions, it becomes evident that sustainable peace and stability can only be achieved through local solutions that prioritise the voices of those directly affected. This understanding calls for a reevaluation of foreign policies and interventions, advocating for a more nuanced approach that supports local autonomy and self-determination.

Dialogue between Saharawi and Moroccan youth emerges as a crucial theme in fostering understanding and cooperation. The younger generation holds the potential to bridge divides and cultivate a shared vision for the future. By engaging in open conversations that address their concerns, aspirations, and experiences, youth from both communities can dismantle stereotypes and build relationships founded on mutual respect. Initiatives that promote exchanges, collaborative projects, and joint advocacy efforts can empower young people to play an active role in shaping a peaceful and inclusive society.

In summary, the themes explored in "Choosing Our Path" collectively reinforce the importance of self-determination, cultural identity, and dialogue in the context of Saharawi and Moroccan communities. Empowering these groups to make their own choices is essential for fostering a sustainable future, free from the constraints of external pressures. As both communities navigate their paths forward, emphasising cultural pride and intergenerational dialogue will be vital in achieving lasting peace and stability in the region.

Foreign intervention has often complicated the dynamics within the region, leading to instability and misunderstanding. External powers may have interests that do not align with the aspirations of the Saharawi and Moroccan peoples, often prioritising geopolitical strategies over genuine human rights and autonomy. By establishing a collaborative approach, both communities can resist external pressures and influence while asserting their right to self-determination. This solidarity can serve as a powerful statement against foreign meddling, emphasising that the future of the region should be shaped by its people, not outside interests.

Engaging in dialogue is essential for the younger generations in both communities. Saharawi and Moroccan youth have the potential to bridge gaps and cultivate understanding through their shared experiences and common goals. Joint initiatives, such as cultural exchanges, educational programs, and community projects, can empower young people to explore their identities while fostering friendships that transcend political divides. By encouraging open communication, both groups can work together to create a sustainable future built on cooperation and mutual respect.

In conclusion, the importance of joint efforts between Saharawi and Moroccan communities lies at the heart of their quest for autonomy and cultural recognition. By prioritising their voices and experiences, they can challenge foreign intervention and pave the way for a more stable and harmonious future. The youth of both communities play a crucial role in this process, as they hold the key to fostering dialogue and understanding. Ultimately, it is through these collaborative efforts that both Saharawi and Moroccan peoples can chart their own path forward, grounded in mutual respect and shared aspirations.

Looking ahead: Hope for Saharawi and Moroccan communities

The future of the Saharawi and Moroccan communities is a landscape rich with potential, where hope can flourish through mutual understanding and collaborative efforts. As both groups navigate the complexities of their historical and cultural identities, it becomes increasingly clear that the path forward lies in the hands of the people directly affected by the ongoing tensions. Empowering local voices is essential, as it allows for authentic representation and self-determination. The communities themselves must take charge of their narratives, seeking solutions that reflect their unique experiences and aspirations rather than those imposed by external forces.

Dialogue is crucial for fostering understanding and cooperation between Saharawi and Moroccan youth. The younger generations are uniquely positioned to bridge divides, armed with fresh perspectives and a desire for peace. Initiatives that encourage interaction, such as cultural exchanges and collaborative projects, can serve as platforms for dialogue. By engaging in open conversations, youth from both sides can dismantle stereotypes and build relationships based on trust and respect. This grassroots approach can lay the groundwork for long-lasting reconciliation, as young leaders emerge to champion shared goals.

Ultimately, the journey towards hope for Saharawi and Moroccan communities hinges on their ability to unite in pursuit of common objectives. By embracing their cultural identities, rejecting foreign intervention, and promoting dialogue among youth, these communities can forge a path towards a more autonomous and harmonious future. It is a call to action for the people of Western Sahara and Morocco to take ownership of their narratives and choices, crafting a narrative that reflects their shared humanity and collective aspirations.

Also by DM Ole Kiminta

How the Western Democracies failed the world
Supporting Refugees in their Homelands
Dissuading Global War Mongers:
Dissuading war mongers
La Libération Monétaire en Afrique
Canada Post: Management failure to modernise mail systems
Canada Post management failure to modernise mail systems
Canada Post: Management failure to modernise mail systems
Live to be 200
Aim to live for 200
Aim to live to be 200
Western democracies failed the world economies
Wrong foot forward: US-Canada trade wars
Canada begs to differ: Never a 51st state of USA
Tethered to the Kitchen
Nous ne pouvons pas être le 51e État des États-Unis
Nous ne serons jamais le 51ème état des États-Unis.
The Nephilim and the erosion of moral boundaries
Every human is an advocate for World Peace
The diplomatic dilemma of Western Sahara
Every human: Advocate for World Peace

About the Author

DM Ole Kiminta is a Canadian of Maasai heritage. He spent many years working in USA, Britain and in Canada. He is an Industrial engineer, Petroleum engineer and Chemical engineer. Ole Kiminta was educated in USA and United Kingdom. Some of his published research work include Material science, carbon fibres and other composite materials, Polymeric materials, and Particle technology. He currently works for the Canadian government and lives in Toronto Canada with his family.

www.ingramcontent.com/pod-product-compliance
Lightning Source LLC
Chambersburg PA
CBHW032116280326
41933CB00009B/867